Understanding Babies and Young Children from Conception to Three

A guide for students, practitioners and parents

Christine Macintyre

 Routledge
Taylor & Francis Group

LONDON AND NEW YORK

First published 2012
by Routledge
2 Park Square, Milton Park, Abingdon, Oxon OX14 4RN

Simultaneously published in the USA and Canada
by Routledge
711 Third Avenue, New York, NY 10017

Routledge is an imprint of the Taylor & Francis Group, an informa business

British Library Cataloguing in Publication Data
A catalogue record for this book is available from the British Library

Library of Congress Cataloging-in-Publication Data
Library of Congress Cataloging-in-Publication Data
Macintyre, Christine, 1938–
Understanding babies and young children from conception to three :
a guide for students, practitioners, and parents / Christine Macintyre.
p. cm.
1. Early childhood education. 2. Child development. I. Title.
LB1139.23.M325 2011
305.231–dc22
2011004646

ISBN: 978–0–415–66977–1 (hbk)
ISBN: 978–0–415–66978–8 (pbk)
ISBN: 978–0–203–80675–3 (ebk)

Typeset in Galliard
by Keystroke, Station Road, Codsall, Wolverhampton

MIX
Paper from
responsible sources
FSC www.fsc.org FSC® C004839

Printed and bound in Great Britain by the MPG Books Group

Understanding Babies and Young Children from Conception to Three

When do bab
What are the
Do movemen
How importa
What can I do

Written to sup   post-
natal develop   ts of
progression d   ne to
influence a ch

Based upon e   lively
to practitioner   t for
quick and easy

- In-depth
- The impo
- The proce
- Early com
- The learni

Other features   tion
research, maki   d in
ongoing profe

This book will   ions
in early years e   ent,
enabling them

Christine Ma   rgh
University, UK   and
abroad. She ha   cial
educational ne

Contents

List of figures

List of tables

Acknowledgements

Thank you to everyone who made this book possible. First, the children who showed how they relished the high-quality teaching and interactions that gave them confidence and challenged their abilities. It was wonderful to see babies thrive, and become crawlers and walkers and talkers. The three-year-olds invariably gave something unexpected to make us smile, and sometimes we had to reconsider the best ways to make their learning environment colourful and appropriate. Very often we had to encourage fantasy play to stimulate their language and communication, and we were fascinated by the scenarios they produced. We gained a real insight into their thinking and what was important for them. We monitored their movement closely, knowing that this was their first language and a key in the process of building attachment and bonding. We included 'tummy time' for the toddlers and many opportunities for crawling, and later climbing and jumping, knowing that these skills would give them confidence and help them to build a high self-esteem.

Thank you to the parents, carers and practitioners/professionals who were willing to share their ideas and concerns through asking questions and waiting patiently for the answers. I know that they all feel their commitment to the children and their parents and carers is so worthwhile, and I hope this book does them justice.

Thank you too to the team at Kirklees – Richard, Kate and Angela who have worked so hard to produce DVDs and booklets of 'The Child's Journey'. Maria Robinson and I were so pleased to play a small part in that huge undertaking. The parents from Kirklees gave permission for their children to be photographed, as did those in the Edinburgh nurseries. My grateful thanks to them all.

I am very grateful to the staff at Taylor & Francis, particularly Alison Foyle and Claire Westwood. I have written many books for them, and they have been so supportive and helpful that I couldn't go anywhere else. And to Diana Chambers who worked meticulously on editing the manuscript. Any remaining mistakes are down to me and I hope you'll be kind.

Acronyms and abbreviations

ADD   Attention Deficit Disorder
ADHD   Attention Deficit Hyperactivity Disorder
EYFS   Early Years Foundation Stage
EYPS   Early Years Professional Status
ID   infant directed
LBW   low birth weight
MRI   magnetic resonance imaging
PET   Positron Emission Topography
RAS   reticular activating system

Introduction

This book has three key aims, all linked to current developments in education. The first is to give 'nature and nurture' information specifically for this age group of children so that all those who have the responsibility of caring for them – i.e. parents, carers and professionals/practitioners in all kinds of settings – gain an enhanced understanding of their development. The second aim, emanating from the first, is to support those who wish to gain further qualifications. Across the UK there is a requirement that teachers and other professionals in the field, such as nursery nurses, nursery managers, social workers and childminders, keep abreast of current research so that their practice facilitates the optimum development of the children in their care. To support this, a range of opportunities to gain different levels of qualification has been provided. These include Foundation degrees, Early Childhood Studies degrees, Social Work and Teaching degrees and EYPS (Early Years Professional Status). They all highlight the link between academic knowledge and practice in the field, and this text is written to provide this kind of information – i.e. to illuminate, 'the individual and diverse ways in which children develop and learn from birth' and 'how children's well-being, development, learning and behaviour can be affected by a range of influences and transitions from inside and outside the setting' (Best Practice Network 2010) EYPS standards document and the Curriculum for Excellence in Scotland (2009) (City of Edinburgh Council 2008). Each of the different qualifications provides enhanced status to the 'takers', and to their settings, for colleagues and parents can be reassured that 'professionals who study' are keen to learn more and are likely to give their children the best start in the long educational journey they must make. The third aim is to encourage practitioners to carry out research in their own settings with their own children. This would allow them to test ideas or form new ones that would then underpin best practice.

While there are other, more general texts on early development, many tend to focus on postnatal development. In contrast, this one begins before birth, i.e. at conception, because that is when 'nature and nurture' begin to influence the developing child. The book then outlines the key aspects of development in a sequential way (covering the development of attachment, communication, movement, learning and language), always acknowledging that development does not occur smoothly, that no two children are the same, and that each one is an active being in a social environment, influenced by different expectations and cultural mores but bringing innate factors such as ability, different temperaments and preferences to each activity. I acknowledge that some of the terminology is quite difficult, but explanations can be found in the Glossary.

The text is written in a question-and-answer format based on questions that have arisen in informal discussions with professionals, parents and carers. Of course, professional parents and professional carers sometimes ask the same questions and at other times put forward another point of view. I have tried to ensure that the material covers everyone's key concerns and so provides the most useful support. I also hope that the text gives a clear and realistic structure that facilitates linking with other texts and research reports, as students are required to do. Potential topics/research questions for students' study are indicated in the text and listed in the Appendix. Obviously, these could be treated at different academic levels appropriate to the interest or qualification being undertaken for observations and recordings can be for private use to monitor the development of just one child and inform the most appropriate next action, or they can study groups of children, or be used in conjunction with the findings from other parents and/or colleagues to compile a small survey. This would fulfil the EYPS S10 criterion, 'Use close and informed observation to monitor children's activity and use this information to improve practice'.

When students are required to undertake research, they are often anxious to find an original topic so that their findings bring a new focus into the academic field. This is quite difficult, but students should understand that their individualised investigation to answer their research question ensures that their findings will produce 'original results' even though the topic for research may have been chosen before. Moreover, this very early time in children's lives is arguably less often researched in the field than school times, and it houses many intriguing possibilities. Suggestions are given in the Appendix, but of course these are only potential starter ideas and there are many, many more. Parents, professionals and carers can select a topic that intrigues them, one that is relevant in their own context. This allows them to widen their horizons, gain greater insights and thus become able to understand and support more children and possibly more families.

Why should professionals need to know about this early time in children's lives? Parents have been named as children's first educators, have they not? Indeed, they have, but in 2011 professionals know they should recognise this critical contribution to the status of the child and they should be keen to build sound relationships with parents so that they can share information and planning to support the child. There is much that professionals can learn from parents and carers if they are willing to explain worries or cultural issues. Many parents would agree that they have not had the opportunity or the time to study child development in detail as the professionals have, or perhaps they were not really interested until they became pregnant or had the responsibility of caring for a young child, and now they would welcome guidance from professionals if it was friendly, appropriate and manageable. So there can be a reciprocal gain. Of course, children are a product of nature and nurture, i.e. what they inherit from their parents (nature), and the people, opportunities and experiences they encounter at home and in the setting (nurture). So understanding both is essential if all the adults are to benefit each of the very different children they will meet.

Researchers over the years – e.g. Ainsworth (1972); Trevarthen (1977); Bee and Boyd (2005); Goddard Blythe (2008); Robinson (2010) – all endorse the claim that the first years are a vitally important time in children's development. This is the time when 'the young brain is thirsting for new information – we are powerless to control it' (Trevarthen 1977), and indeed practitioners constantly strive to satisfy this urge by providing the best opportunities for learning. These years house the most critical times for sensory and motor development, as well as the intellectual and social aspects, and they are also the times when experiences begin to impact on children's self-esteem. In these early times, the children begin to build a sense of who they are and add to that their judgements of how able they are. This is so important both for forming relationships and friendships, and for acquiring the confidence and the competences that enable them to cope positively with all the activities of daily living both at home, at nursery or children's and families' centres, and eventually at school.

The individual differences observed in children's development raise intriguing questions about how, when and why they arose, and finding the answers stimulates fascinating pieces of research. Are these differences laid-down differences at conception? If so, is much of development pre-set? Or, if not, when and in what ways does the environment impact on development? Is nature or nurture the most powerful tool and if, as commonly expressed, development is a blend of the two, which is more prevalent at what age and in what ways can one compensate for any disadvantage in the other?

To understand such questions, the pre-birth and neonatal environments must be explored to find what happens when. This book raises issues such as 'What can mothers-to-be do to give the developing foetus the best chance?' and 'In this very first environment, the womb, what **teratogens** affect the unborn child?' The birth process itself leads to different influences on the child's well-being and leads to questions such as 'What are the benefits of a vaginal birth for both mother and child?'

All the developmental processes that are genetic/innate or learned by experiences in the environment are also the sources for the questions and answers in the book, e.g. if mothers and babies do not immediately bond, what then? Will there be a long-lasting effect? Such questions are considered in the text by reference to current research, e.g. Bee and Boyd (2005), Robinson (2010), Winston (2004). Where there are no definite outcomes, this is stated so that readers appreciate that ongoing findings can provide conflicting results and that research may not provide firm answers. These anomalies might hold the spark for further investigations. As just one example, the question of the best way to promote language is disputed by those who believe in the soft melodic tones of motherese and those who prefer mothers to talk to their babies in adult language from the start. Professionals may be intrigued by the differences and wish to research such issues in their own settings.

The aforementioned researchers also show that if these critical learning times are missed, then skills and competences may not be recaptured, or they may be much harder to acquire. Specifically referring to the development of language, Winston (2004) claims, 'at birth we are all international, yet by three, we have tuned in to the sounds of our mother tongue making it much, much harder to learn another tongue'.

The poet, teacher and author Peter Dixon (2005) in his wonderful book, *Let Me Be*, explains how this period must be given prominence in its own right, not only as a preparation time for later. He recommends that all children have much more time for play and imaginative activities, making choices, and he reassures adults that through such experiences they are much more likely to build a positive sense of self. He urges those who disbelieve, i.e. those who see childhood mainly as a preparation for adulthood, to get their zimmers out and practise now – just in case.

I hope you will find the study as intriguing as I do and that this book will help you to understand children better and enjoy them more. I think people who have the responsibility of caring for children have the best, if the most complex job in the world. Over many years I have met hundreds of committed early years practitioners who think so too, and this book is a tribute to them. After all, as I say in all my books, 'it is to the young that the future belongs'.

I know that people can be offended by being labelled with the 'wrong' title. However, it is very cumbersome to write 'parents, carers, practitioners and professionals' all of the time. Please believe that if I have used the wrong title, I mean no disrespect and ask you to forgive me.

Chapter 1

The earliest development
From conception to birth

Conceiving a baby, nurturing a baby, giving birth, then guiding the child through toddlerhood and early childhood are different stages in what should be a wonderful process. It is certainly awe-inspiring and exciting as well as daunting. For, of course, alongside the pleasurable anticipations, parents, especially first-time parents, have many questions, e.g. 'What happens during my baby's development both before and after birth?', 'What do I need to know about babies?', 'What can I do to give my baby the best start in life?' and even 'Who determines whether it is a boy or a girl?' Often parents think ahead and wonder, 'Will the things our baby inherits from us influence how they will grow and learn and behave?' These are vitally important concerns and this chapter will set out to answer questions like these so that parents, professionals and other carers may understand the sequence of events that bring bodily and lifestyle changes for mothers, babies and indeed the whole family. This understanding will support professionals in recognising how family events can impact on the behaviour and learning of the children in their setting. The information will also help them to know what planning and timing of input is most appropriate. In this way they can ensure that each child has the best possible start in life.

Professionals who will share in the care and education of young children have many questions, too. Much of the literature on early childhood development (e.g. Bee and Boyd 2005) claims that babies learn even before they are born. So questions such as 'How can this be and what are they learning? And in what ways does this early learning contribute to competence later on?' need to be answered. Professionals, who form key parts of the 'nurture' scenario for little children, are always fascinated by the perennial questions that source many pieces of research, for example, 'What parts do nature and nurture play in children's development and how does one influence the other?' These kinds of 'educational' questions are very similar to those posed by the parents and they show how professionals, who will hopefully be working together with the parents, need to understand the developmental process from the very start.

Such understandings are also the foundation stones of strong parent/professional relationships. These develop through professionals getting to know and respect the family and the home environment as well as the child, while the family in turn builds relationships that allow them to frankly share joys or concerns about their child's progress. When confidence and trust are established, professionals may well be asked to give advice on the 'best ways' of supporting the child's learning at home. How can they do this if they have not learned about the experiences the parents have had and understood the child's background? It is also important that professionals understand and respect the relative contributions that homes and settings make towards the children's optimum development. In this light they are enabled to communicate appropriately with the parents in terms of their cultural, social and economic mores.

Those who are embarking on further academic study will have more questions, e.g. 'In what ways is an academic study enriched by studying life before birth?' One brief answer to this must be that the observations professionals make of children in their care are enhanced by understandings of how they come to be as they are, and this might mean appreciating the effects of birth traumas or disabilities. Learning is a lifelong process and when professionals become involved, it has already begun. They need to recognise what very different children know and understand and consider that in context, i.e. in relation to the life experiences the children have had. This is the best basis for planning new individual challenges and experiences, and interventions. On a more personal level, they need to appreciate where the children are coming from, i.e. the background and expectations of their particular culture, if they are to respond to them respectfully.

So, let's begin and discover what questions parents and carers and professionals ask. First-time mother-to-be Lisa wonders:

Q: What actually happens at conception? How does the baby develop in the earliest days? How important is the environment in supporting the child?

A: There are really three questions here. Let's look at conception first and then we'll talk about early development and the first environment, the womb.

The first step in the development of a baby happens at conception when a single sperm cell from the millions the father produces at ejaculation pierces the wall of the **ovum** from the mother. A new life begins.

The mother only produces one egg cell per month from one of her two ovaries. This happens midway between two menstrual periods. If the egg cell is not fertilised, it travels from the ovary down the **fallopian tube** and disintegrates, to be flushed away at the next period. If intercourse occurs during the vital few days when the ovum is in the fallopian tube, a single sperm will travel through the women's vagina, cervix, uterus and fallopian tube before penetrating the wall of the ovum. This results in a child being conceived, although only about half of that number will survive to birth.

Q: I understand that conception happens when the sperm and egg merge and the resulting pregnancy lasts for nine months. Is the baby safely in the womb from the moment of conception?

A: Conception takes place two weeks after a menstrual period and the time from then to the baby's birth is 265 days. The developmental changes that occur over that time are caused by an inbuilt or innate maturational timetable. Most doctors will talk about pregnancy lasting

40 weeks (i.e. taking the date from the date of the last period), but there are really 38 weeks gestation from the point of conception.

These 38 weeks are subdivided into three stages that GPs usually call trimesters. New mothers-to-be are often wary of spreading the news of the impending arrival until the first trimester is safely over because then they feel the baby has safely taken hold. They may also be aware that many fertilised ova do not survive and that miscarriages are relatively common in the early weeks. In fact, many women can miscarry without having realised they were pregnant.

Embryologists, however, tend to subdivide the 38 weeks according to the three stages of development.

Q: Three stages? What are they?

A: These are the germinal stage, the embryonic stage and the foetal stage.

At the germinal stage, in the first 24–36 hours after conception in the fallopian tube (see Figure 1.1), cell division begins and in two or three days a clump of undifferentiated cells the size of a pinhead appears. Four days or so later, this organism, now named the **blastocyst**, begins to subdivide and separates into two rings. The outer ring of cells forms the support structures for the baby and the inner ring of cells forms the **embryo** itself. As this occurs, the cell ring travels along the fallopian tube and enters the uterus. There, the outer ring of cells in the blastocyst on contact with the uterus opens and tendrils attach themselves to the uterine wall. This process is called implantation.

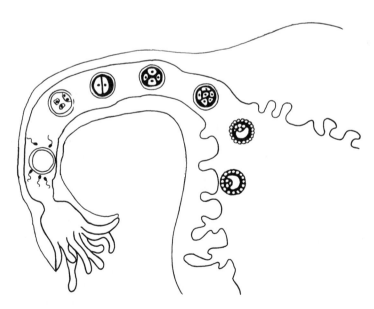

Figure 1.1 The first ten days of gestation

The embryonic stage lasts for six to ten weeks after implantation. This is the time when the support structures develop. Two critically important ones are the **amnion**, a sac filled with amniotic fluid in which the developing foetus grows, and the **placenta**, a mass of cells that lies against the uterus. The placenta is formed very early and carries out the functions of the liver, lungs and kidneys for the embryo and later, the foetus.

Q: So are there still hazards or is the pregnancy safe now?

A: There are still potential problems, depending on the mother's lifestyle. This is why ongoing advice about not smoking or taking drugs is in all the magazines and leaflets at the medical centres.

Q: What happens when there are challenging lifestyles?

A: Well, the **umbilical cord** connects the circulatory system to the placenta and it acts as a bridge and a filter, supplying the foetus with nutrients from the mother's blood and taking waste matter back so that the mother can eliminate it. This filter is critical because it acts as a safety net. Unfortunately, some viruses do pass through and they attack the placenta, reducing the supply of nutrients to the developing embryo. However, other viruses are too large and are eliminated by the mother. Some drugs, alcohol and some illnesses also pass through and these impact on the baby's well-being. This is why mothers are encouraged to adopt the healthiest diet and lifestyle possible before conception and at all times during pregnancy.

In the past, it was thought that most 'negatives' or harmful substances were filtered out. **Rubella**, a form of measles, has been known to be potentially harmful to the baby's hearing and vision if the mother caught the illness in the first three months when the baby was developing fast. Later in the pregnancy, catching this illness did not have the same effect – the timing of the infection was critical. This understanding led to girls being vaccinated against German measles by their sixteenth birthday. Mostly, however, it was thought that the baby cushioned in the womb was 'safe', taking all its necessary requirements from the mother. An old saying was 'lose a tooth for every child', suggesting that the embryo 'took' all the necessary calcium and left mothers with toothache.

Nowadays, the effects of alcohol, smoking and drug taking during pregnancy may be seen in the newborn child, proving that the filter is not totally effective and that many harmful substances, e.g. cocaine, find their way into the baby's developing systems. In extreme cases newborns can have **foetal alcohol syndrome**, one of the most common causes of intellectual retardation. Others have to go through drug withdrawal and suffer fitting and tremors and subsequent communication and/or learning difficulties. 'About a third of all cocaine exposed babies are born prematurely; they have **low birth weight** and show significant withdrawal symptoms after birth' (Hawley and Disney 1992: 1–22). The long-term effects are still being researched.

Q: When does the heart begin to beat?

A: At four weeks' gestation, there is a heartbeat even though the embryo is only about 2in. (5cm) long (Bee and Boyd 2005). The embryo itself is forming by differentiating the initial mass of cells into specialist groups that will become skin, nerve cells and sensory receptors, internal organs, muscles and the circulatory system itself. Eyes and ears are beginning to be formed, the mouth can open and close, and there is a primitive spinal column.

The foetal stage, when the nervous system develops, lasts for the remaining seven months, and this is the time when systems and structures are refining and strengthening (see Table 1.1 below). The nervous system develops most at this stage. During foetal development the brain develops bulb-like at the upper end of the neural tube that forms the spine (Carter 2000). The main sections of the brain, including the cerebral **cortex**, can be seen at seven weeks after conception and by birth the baby will have 100 billion neurons. However, these neurons are not yet mature, so they don't have the capacity to communicate with one another to make things happen. **Maturation** is the sorting of the neurons into similar groups that can work together to achieve some end.

In potential premature births paediatricians do their utmost to keep the baby in the womb until at least 28 weeks. This is because the nervous system and other vital organs are viable then and so babies are likely to avoid developmental difficulties.

Q: How is the genetic material from each parent passed on?

A: Unless there is a genetic abnormality or an accident in cell division, the nucleus of each cell in the body will contain **46 chromosomes** arranged in 23 pairs and these carry all the genetic or inherited information. The sperm and the egg are different, however. These specialised cells, called **gametes**, have a final divisive stage (**meiosis**) in which each new cell receives only one chromosome from the original pair. So each gamete has 23 chromosomes, not 23 pairs. The sperm brings the genetic material from the father and the egg contains the mother's genetic endowment; these combine to form the 23 pairs that will be part of each cell in the new baby. In other pregnancies this material will be different. This means that each baby has a unique genetic blueprint that will influence what they will be able to do. Parents often exclaim that their children are 'as different as chalk and cheese' and the reason why this is true is because in subsequent pregnancies, each child will have inherited a **genotype** all of their own.

The genotype (i.e. the specific set of instructions contained in the genes) holds the child's individual characteristics such as body build, hair colour, some aspects of intelligence, and temperamental traits such as **resilience** or vulnerability, shyness or outgoingness, or **extra-version**. Some learning difficulties can be inherited too, e.g. dyslexia, **dyspraxia** or autism, and children can be born with a propensity to some illnesses, but it is by no means certain that these will develop. Knowing the possibility of serious illness, however, should encourage potential parents to be tested and being aware of the signs can allow them to seek immediate medical help should the need arise.

The **phenotype**, on the other hand, is the set of characteristics observed after birth and is a product of the genotype, i.e. the nature side of development, the environmental influences from the time of conception (the nurture side) and the interaction of the two. So, although a child could have a genotype for special gifts or talents, this potential could be damaged by the mother taking drugs during her pregnancy. As a result, her child could become a low achiever. This is why the quality of the first and subsequent environments is critically important and why all mothers should take steps to ensure that they give their baby the best possible start.

Q: Is there a timetable for prenatal development? Is this why scans are done?

A: The prenatal timetable (see Table 1.1) is the same for all children in all cultures, and scans provide a way of checking that prenatal development is proceeding well.

Q: Who determines the sex of the baby? My partner is anxious to have a daughter. If we had a son, would my partner be to blame, he wonders?

A: Earlier, we spoke about the 23 pairs of chromosomes that were paired in each of our cells. In 22 of the pairs, the chromosomes look alike and have the same genetic content. In the

Table 1.1 The earliest sequence of development

Gestational age	Key developmental changes
12 weeks	The sex of the baby can be discovered: toes and fingers can be seen and eyelids and lips are formed.
16 weeks	Although the baby has been moving for some time, mothers now feel the movements and can be surprised by the strength of the kicks. Limbs are strengthening and ears are formed.
20 weeks	The baby looks like a miniature of self now – hair is growing and limbs are lengthening. The baby may even begin to suck a thumb or finger.
24 weeks	The baby is now capable of breathing if born at this stage, but survival rates are low. The baby can taste and may be aware of sounds, but cannot see – eyes are formed but closed. There is no light in the womb to stimulate vision.
28 weeks	The nervous system can function now. Babies still lack fat and, after birth, some may have breathing and digestive problems until their systems mature. At this stage babies can survive, especially well if womb-like conditions can be sustained, e.g. incubators providing constant warmth, feeding by tube and extra oxygen/medicinal drugs given to support underdeveloped lungs.
–> 40 weeks	Babies gain muscle strength, fat and all systems are in place.

remaining pair, however, the sex chromosomes are different and are usually referred to as the X and Y chromosomes.

A female has two X (XX) chromosomes on the 23rd pair and a male has an X and a Y, i.e. an (XY) pattern. The mother has only X chromosomes and the father has XY. So when the father's gametes divide, half the sperm will carry an X and half a Y chromosome. If the sperm that fertilises the egg carries an X chromosome, the baby will have an XX pattern and be a girl; if the sperm carries a Y chromosome, the baby will have an XY pattern and be a boy.

Q: What about twins – what happens then?

A: Most births are of single babies but 1:100 births produces twins. The most usual is fraternal twins when more than one egg has been produced and each has been fertilised by a different sperm. These twins are no more alike than any other two babies except, of course, that they have shared the same prenatal environment and experienced the same pattern of nurture within the family. They may well be different in sex, in body build and in temperament, just like other siblings.

In contrast, there are identical twins, but this is a much less common occurrence. Here, a single fertilised egg divides and each half becomes an individual, but because they have inherited the same genetic pattern they will be identical. This does not mean that they will think alike. 'Thanks to the infinitely complex interplay of nature and nurture no two brains are exactly the same. Even identical twins have different brains by the time they are born because the tiny difference in the foetal environment of each is enough to affect their development' (Carter 2000: 17).

Nature and nurture: how do they affect twins?

Often twins reared together and apart are used in research to try to discover the relative importance of nature and nurture. It is fascinating that identical twins, even those separated at birth and reared apart until they are reunited in adulthood, retain many similar features and preferences. This would indicate the strength of genetic inheritance withstanding environmental influences. Interesting, too, is the fact that although the twins may have been nurtured in very different homes, their IQ scores remain similar (Brody 1992). As expected, identical twins brought up together in the same environment have very similar IQ scores, much more so than fraternal twins in the same circumstance. Identical twins reared apart are remarkably similar also, although less so than if they had been reared together. Also in adopted babies, the IQ score is nearer to that of the biological mother than the adoptive one. Such findings make a fascinating and revealing study, one that professionals in settings could research through observing and recording the preferences or temperaments or rates of progress of each twin.

Q: Does this mean that the quality of the environment is less important than what children inherit from their parents?

A: The nature/nurture debate has been raging for many years. This is because it is so difficult to separate the effects of the two. Although the genotype carries the genes, from conception the developing embryo and thereafter the foetus are being affected by the quality of their first environment within the womb. The nurturance of the **placenta**, what passes through the umbilical cord, the nutrients the developing baby receives and whether teratogens (i.e. diseases or chemicals that affect the unborn baby at the critical time) are present, are all key influencing factors.

Carter (2000: 18) claims that 'the uterine environment has a profound effect on the wiring of a baby's brain' and that life in the womb shows how genes and the environment are inextricably linked. She explains that the male foetus has genes that stimulate the production of hormones, including testosterone, at certain times in the brain's development. This in effect makes the brain more masculine and in so doing promotes the differences that are typically seen in the developmental prowess between girls and boys, e.g. girls are better at early fine motor skills and boys are better at tasks that require spatial awareness. Another interesting finding is that babies born to mothers who have enjoyed curry during their pregnancy take readily to spicy foods as if they were already accustomed to the taste.

Another consideration that prevents undisputed nature/nurture claims is that researchers are bound by ethical codes. This means that their investigations cannot deprive a child of any positive input in order to provide research data (Macintyre 2002a), so it is difficult to control impinging variables to pinpoint cause and effect, especially in interactions that happen from conception onwards.

Q: You mentioned the child's temperament. Surely, traits such as shyness or vulnerability can be influenced by the child's upbringing? Isn't that what parenting and education at nursery are all about?

A: Influenced, yes, but temperamental traits are quite enduring. This means that while parents can encourage their sensitive or reluctant-to-participate children to be more confident and outgoing through having consistent expectations and 'rules', and through giving praise and being constantly supportive, in times of stress or new experiences, children tend to revert to their inherited mode of behaviour. The tentative ones are very likely always to need a little more time and reassurance than naturally outgoing children would. Indeed, two children with very different inherited traits, undergoing the same experience, could perceive it differently and this would affect their reactions to it. Think of an impulsive child and a reflective one visiting a fairground. The impulsive child would leap on to the rides with no thought or worry about 'how fast' or 'how high' the rides would go, while the reflective child would hang back, contemplating the pros and cons and be much less liable to take risks. While this reaction could be changed by the children's previous experience of a funfair and what had happened then, their spontaneous reaction to novel experiences is modified by their inherited temperamental traits. Pointing out the implications of behaving in certain ways could help children appreciate different outcomes and discussions about confronting hypothetical new situations. It could also be valuable once the children are mature enough to adjust to such reactions; particularly in the young child, the inherited potential is strong. Bee and Boyd (2005: 17) call this 'experience filtered through biases'.

Q: Is having one temperamental trait better than another?

A: There are times when impulsivity is best, e.g. when quick decisions are required and at other times reflection is more useful in order to make rational decisions or even just to save bumps and bruises. Gradually, over time and with guidance, most children learn to use the most appropriate way to suit the circumstance. Impulsivity does tend to diminish with maturity and this allows reflection and selection of the best ways of behaving. This explains why young children need most supervision, for they may well act without considering the consequences of tumbling down a slope or even drinking bleach. Later, as they gain control – a maturational process – and experiences expand, it is hoped they will slow down and become safely independent. When they do, it shows that nature and nurture are working together to provide the best outcome.

Q: If children have clever parents, have they a greater chance of being clever?

A: This is a key question that always features in the nature/nurture debate and is one for which it is difficult to give an unequivocal answer. This is because children have their own agenda as well as their inherited potential, and this may work with or go against the parents' plans. It is very difficult to motivate a child who is a reluctant learner or not interested in the task at hand, no matter what the learning potential is. So the outcome of the parents' wish list – should that be high achievement – cannot be guaranteed.

Having said that, research shows that parents who have high IQ scores themselves are more likely to provide a more stimulating environment for their children who may already have 'done well' in terms of their inherited potential for learning. The signs are favourable. However, as already mentioned, the children themselves may lack the motivation, the confidence or commitment to make the most of their auspicious start. Extrovert children, even those in less advantaged homes, ask more questions; they explore their environment more and set up opportunities for more problem solving. In so doing they are enhancing what they have been given. Even in the earliest months, children who are difficult to involve or those who Thomas and Chess (1977) describe as 'slow-to-warm-up' do not invite the same level of interaction by giving smiles or other overtures, so they may be denied the time and stimulation that others receive.

Horowitz (1987) conceptualised a model that has stood the test of time. She explained that a resilient child in a poor environment could do well since that child would seek out stimulation and take advantage of all the opportunities that became available. A vulnerable child, she claimed, might also do well if the environment provided constant care and stimulus. However, the vulnerable child in a poor environment, i.e. one who is doubly disadvantaged, suffers most and poor outcomes are sure to follow. Does this help to clarify how inherited and environmental factors interact?

Q: Jack was anxious that his son would be bigger than he was. Wryly smiling, he remembered 'always sitting, legs crossed in the front row in the school photo'. Would that be his son's fate too?

A: Body build is another inherited factor that can cause pleasure or anguish. Children's height is affected mainly by their genes but also (less so) by their environment. This is why height is taken as a measure of general health. If there is no underlying illness, children who fail to grow well may be showing evidence of malnutrition or emotional deprivation (Tanner 1990). However, no amount of wishing will make a tall person small or the other way around. So a child who grows too tall to fulfil his dream of being a jockey or a short child who wants to be a basketball player just has to make other plans. Generally speaking, however, there is reversion to the mean. Children of tall parents tend not to get taller and taller, although looking at height patterns in the new generation, it might seem that they do. Also, children of short parents may outgrow them. Part of being a parent involves calmly waiting to see how their children develop.

Certainly, diet can make children slim or fat, but if this were the sole determining factor, we wouldn't have children with huge appetites who stay surprisingly slender. These children have inherited a metabolic rate that will burn up calories. Again, the nature/nurture interaction is important, because fat cells laid down in the first years can be hard to shift later on. Sadly, images of stick thin models in the media may prevent children from eating enough to keep them healthy, but this shouldn't be a worry in the first three years.

Q: I've heard of dominant and recessive genes. What is the difference and what kind of influence could they have?

A: Let's take curly hair as one example. At the moment, this is out of fashion and not regarded as the huge benefit it once was. Curly hair is controlled by a dominant gene, so a child needs to inherit this from only one parent to have curly hair. On the other hand, straight hair is controlled by a recessive gene, so to avoid having to buy straighteners, the child must inherit a straight hair gene from both parents. If only one parent passes on a straight hair gene, the child will have curls but may pass on a straight hair gene to her own children.

Of course, this transmission is much more significant when it comes to passing on serious diseases such as Huntingdon's chorea, which is not usually diagnosed until adulthood. This is passed on through dominant genes and today a blood test can reveal whether an adult will or will not develop the disease. As Huntingdon's affects both intellectual and motor functions, its presence may well affect an adult's decision to have children and risk passing it on to a new generation. Without early knowledge of its presence and transmission, however, a couple may unwittingly keep the gene alive.

Q: There have been several mentions of critical times. What are these?

A: While some teratogens (harmful factors such as smoking, alcohol and other drugs) can affect the developing child at any time during pregnancy, most have critical times when the effect is most powerful. If the mother catches rubella or German measles during the first three months of pregnancy, then the baby will suffer some damage. However, if the disease is caught beyond that period, no harm results. The first eight weeks are the most vulnerable times for the development of the organ systems (Moore and Persaud 1993). A disease or illness in the mother beyond that time will not have the same devastating effect on the baby's kidneys, liver or heart. However, the nervous system is most at risk in the second half of the pregnancy because that is the time when it is developing most rapidly.

Critical periods influence development after birth, too. One blind ten-year-old underwent a new eye operation believing that he would be able to see. Although the operation was technically perfect, the child did not gain sight. The optic nerves had not been stimulated at the right time, i.e. the critical learning time. It was too late (Winston 2004). (See also critical times in learning language on p. 94.) For the same reason, untreated hearing problems such as glue ear may result in longlasting speech/spelling/reading difficulties because the child has not heard the sounds of their own language clearly at the critical time.

Q: Do babies actually learn in the womb? This seems very strange. How can they do that?

A: The question of when learning begins is a fascinating one. New research shows that children are listening and learning even before they are born. Eleanor Winner in her television programme *The Brilliant Brain* claims that 'at birth we have already been listening for twelve weeks'. This would seem to be confirmed when expectant mothers tell of their babies becoming still when they listen to them repeating nursery rhymes or playing favourite pieces of music. However, this does not mean, as has been claimed, that playing Mozart to unborn children will result in them becoming talented musicians. At this early stage they do not have the neurological maturation to allow this to happen. In addition, as babies kick in the womb they are learning about distances and directions, so developing their kinaesthetic and proprioceptive senses. They are also stimulating their **vestibular sense**, or sense of balance, that will help them get into the head-down position ready for a vaginal birth. They are also discovering their body boundary, i.e. where they end and the outside world begins. This will transfer into spatial awareness and impact on the child's positive sense of self and in turn their self-esteem (Macintyre 2009b).

Scans of babies' faces when they are given new tastes show that pre-birth, they already have likes and dislikes. So the new baby is far from being a blank slate or helpless, as was previously claimed. Some sensory learning has begun and will develop very quickly in the weeks after birth so that almost from the start, the baby is a social being.

Q: What about the mother's diet? How important is that?

A: When a mother is severely malnourished during pregnancy, as happens in underprivileged or war-zone countries, the risks of a stillbirth or a baby dying during the first year are greatly increased. A very poor diet in the last three months seems particularly linked to tragic outcomes, and even surviving babies born into conditions like these may die from infections and illnesses that a more robust child would throw off. These children will lack energy and so be less responsive to their environment. Those who lack stimulation may revert to rocking and have blank, unseeing expressions. One example are the babies in the orphanages of Romania who had a poor prenatal diet and little postnatal stimulation.

Q: What about weight gain?

A: The current advice is that mothers should gain 25–35lb (11–16kg) during the nine months and there are optimum times for weight gain. In the first trimester the weight gain should only be around 5lb (2.2kg). The major gain should be in the last six months in order to support the growing foetus. The increased food should be protein. A cup of cottage cheese will provide 1oz (33g) of protein and an egg ¼oz (7g), so the advised extra 2½oz (75g) per day is relatively easy to obtain. Fish, especially oily fish which contains omega 3, is recommended, and calcium intake should increase to encourage the formation of strong bones and teeth. Supplementary iron to enrich the blood and folic acid may be recommended by the GP as well, because the latter can reduce the risk of neural tube defects such as spina bifida.

Boys need five times the amount of zinc in utero for the formation of the testes. Gross deficiency may also lead to delayed development and, more subtly, to poor communication between mother and child (Keen and Hurely 1989). Many children who have Attention Deficit Hyperactivity Disorder (ADHD) have low levels of zinc, and, generally speaking, there are many more boys who develop ADHD at an earlier age. Zinc deficiency can even affect children's eating habits. Those who insist on bland foods may experience this lack.

Q: So it is only boys who are affected?

A: Zinc deficiencies show up later in girls, most usually around age ten, when the girls are approaching puberty. Zinc regulates the hormones and low zinc has been related to eating disorders such as anorexia (Bee 1995).

Q: I never knew zinc was so important. What can we do to replenish it?

A: Zinc is needed for healing, especially in skin conditions such as eczema. I wonder who remembers how effective 'zinc and castor oil' cream was for nappy rash? Today, zinc bandages are often used to cool and calm eczema. Stressed babies and mothers will use up more zinc, so keeping calm brings benefits to both mother and child. Wholegrain foods such as cereals are a good source of zinc, so diet makes a big difference to well-being.

Q: Smoking seems mild after all those other negatives? What effect does this have?

A: Smoking is harmful. Mothers who smoke during pregnancy are allowing their babies to ingest the negative effects of tobacco, i.e. carbon monoxide and nicotine. Nicotine constricts the vessels supplying blood to the placenta and carbon monoxide reduces the supply of oxygen to the soft tissues of the body, resulting in fewer nutrients reaching the foetus. The babies may be born too soon and suffer the difficulties of prematurity. Even full-term babies tend to be smaller and this may affect their subsequent growth, not only in physical aspects but in intellectual and social development too. There is also a greater risk of miscarriage and respiratory difficulties in the newborn baby. Practising yoga or having a massage can help to reduce stress and replace the effects of tobacco.

So there are many decisions to be made beyond the baby's name and the colour of the nursery walls. However, with care, nature sees that the reproductive system is robust and it will tolerate some 'slips' in lifestyle. Better, however, for mothers to avoid all substances that might cause harm and so take no chances of affecting the baby at all.

Q: What about the mother's age? More mothers are having their children later. Is this harmful? And how does the age factor impact on teenagers?

A: There are many reasons for delaying pregnancy, but increased risks must be considered too. Research suggests that mothers over 30 and particularly over 35 have more chance of complications during pregnancy, including late pregnancy miscarriage, particularly if they have had inadequate prenatal care. Current research suggests that the best time for child-bearing is in the early 20s and that delayed childbearing poses risks for both mother and baby, even when prenatal care has been good (Bee and Boyd 2005).

The benefits and difficulties encountered by teenage mothers-to-be are still being researched, but if they have adequate prenatal care, difficulties are much less common than with older mothers. Difficulties seem to be due to poor prenatal care rather than the age of the teenage mother itself.

> Q: The mother's age is often linked to having a baby with **Down's syndrome?** Is this true?

A: Down's syndrome is caused by a genetic error and/or an accident in cell division later on. Instead of the baby receiving 46 chromosomes, it receives an extra chromosome (three copies of chromosome 21) and this causes both the physical and intellectual difficulties associated with the condition. The likelihood of this happening increases with age. There are prenatal tests to determine the presence of the syndrome that lead to difficult decisions about termination, because many children with Down's can lead happy, fulfilled lives and many are socially charming. Aaron (2006) has identified a gene benefit particular to this condition and the resulting sociability in the children can bring much happiness to a family. Although children with Down's syndrome will not be high achievers in intellectual terms, many can do much better than previously thought possible if they are given support and a visual curriculum in a mainstream school that understands their condition. Sue Buckley, championing inclusion for children with Down's syndrome in Portsmouth, has proved that, in a school where staff are committed to inclusion and are willing to understand the condition and prepare a visual curriculum to ease the children's learning, children with the condition can thrive. Later, young adults can be independent, possibly in a sheltered occupation. It is very likely, however, that they will need extra care and support throughout their lives.

Some parents, especially older ones, may feel unable to make this commitment and terminate the pregnancy or choose adoption. Much depends on family circumstances, religious beliefs, and previous experiences and understanding of Down's syndrome. Some children, of course, are more severely affected than others with complex heart problems and other medical conditions requiring treatments and operations.

No outsider can make decisions for any parents as to what they do and when they do it, but many are seeking advice as to how their baby can have the optimum start in life and hopefully this will allow them to make choices that make them and their baby healthy and happy. Is there anything more important than that?

Birth and the newborn child

The long-awaited time is here. The baby is ready to be born and all the preparations have been made. Yet there is always some anxiety in case the birth process itself causes the mother or baby harm or pain, for both mothers and babies work hard during the birth process. Babies have large heavy heads in relation to their size (twice the size of an adult's head) and the size of the mother's pelvis is limited by her upright posture. This is not an auspicious start, yet the vaginal delivery has benefits missing in the **Caesarian section** delivery, which is sometimes necessary due to blood pressure or other medical problems or demanded by those, in common parlance who are 'too posh to push'. Perhaps they have other pressing concerns.

The birth canal is not the same width all the way down and, to accommodate the large head, the baby must twist and turn to be born. So full-term babies who are in the correct head-down position (showing that their sense of balance is working well) and have the most strength are off to the best start. Nature has also provided full-term babies with a number of primitive **reflexes** to help them in their birth process.

Q: What are the benefits of a normal delivery? When I had my first baby, I said 'Never again' and when no. 2 was due, I was determined to have a C-section [Caesarian section], but that wasn't allowed. Why not?

A: During a vaginal birth, the contractions that give the mother pain and at the end the powerful urge to push, are massaging the baby and helping it to clear its lungs ready for independent breathing (Goddard Blythe 2008: 52). Pressure on the baby's head also stimulates the production of hormones (e.g. thyroid, adrenaline) and these help the babies control their temperature as they leave the warmth of the womb and enter the colder world. They also work to prevent the babies breathing too soon and ingesting substances from the birth canal. Babies born naturally also have their immune systems boosted, which is important for withstanding new bacteria. Some studies, e.g. Oslo Public Health 2005, have found that C-section babies tend to be more prone to allergies and food intolerances. But the major risk for babies born by C-section is breathing problems. Bennett and Brown (1989) explain why. They write:

> During a vaginal delivery 110 ml of lung fluid is present within the respiratory tract. During delivery, compression of the chest wall assists in the expulsion of this fluid. Infants delivered by c-section are denied the benefits of chest compression and expression of lung fluid.

So babies may find breathing difficult and require extra support.

The vaginal birth baby has many pros, therefore. What about the mother? Is it best for her? Usually, once the baby is born all memories of the discomfort disappear and recovery is much quicker. A C-section scar can be painful for some time and hinder lifting the baby. Sometimes it's just not as easy as it seems.

Q: What about the way the baby is lying?

A: The way the baby presents or lies in the womb has a big influence on the birth process. The ideal position is when the baby's head is down, with the head forward and the chin tucked in. The foetal head exerts pressure on the cervix, which must dilate to let the baby through. The pressure stimulates the secretion of **oxytocin**. This hormone stimulates the contractions for the birth of the baby and then the ejection of the placenta. It also helps in the projection of milk and so supports bonding.

A breech presentation (3–4 per cent of babies lie this way) is when the baby exits 'bottom first'. Often midwives try to rotate the baby into the head-down position but sometimes the baby won't budge or reverts to the original position. This is unfortunate because the baby's bottom does not give the same pressure on the cervix as the harder head, so labour may be longer. The breech position may indicate that the baby' s sense of balance is not functioning well at this stage. There are many breech babies who go on to have no difficulties at all, but in the population of children who do have specific learning needs such as dyspraxia, a disproportionate number have had breech births (Macintyre 2009a).

Delivery

Delivery has three stages. The first is called the onset and describes the period from the start of contractions until the cervix is dilated enough for the baby's head to pass through. This is usually the longest stage, lasting between 12 and 19, even 24 hours for a first baby, although the contractions at the start are quite mild. The second stage has the actual delivery of the baby – the stage when the mother can push to help her baby be born.

Great care is taken to prevent tearing of the tissues at this stage. Sometimes an episiotomy is done to give the baby more room to emerge and to make 'sewing up' more straightforward. The third stage is the delivery of the placenta or afterbirth and other materials from the **uterus**.

> Q: What about birth weight? Is there an ideal and why should that be?

A: In 2010 anecdotal evidence seems to show that full-term newborns are getting bigger, with some over 10lb. Contrast that with the low birth-weight babies (LBW) who weigh in at 3lb or even less. All babies below 5lb are described as LBW and there are different causes of this start to life that may require intensive therapy and separation from the mother for a while.

The most common cause of prematurity is that the babies are born before full term (38 weeks of gestation). Sometimes high blood pressure or other illnesses make early delivery advisable. Hospitals try to keep the baby in the womb until 28 weeks because the lungs and other systems have a key time for maturing. However, full-term babies can be very small, too. These would be called small-for-date babies. These babies may have suffered from pre-natal malnutrition due to the mother smoking and so constricting blood flow, or from other significant prenatal problems. These babies are more at risk of developing problems later but, of course, nothing is set in stone. Many do very well. Alternatively, preterm infants are early but have been developing normally in other respects, so there is no neurological damage. However, paediatricians do try to keep them in the womb until 28 weeks gestation because all the major organs and the nervous system are functioning fully by then.

All LBW babies are less responsive at birth and many experience respiratory distress in the first weeks. Some may reach their motor milestones later and some go on to show learning difficulties, but long-term outcomes depend on a variety of factors, e.g. how small the baby was, the quality of the neonatal care and the type of support given by the family once the baby goes home. This is another quandary for those who seek to research the nature/nurture debate.

Recent technological developments, creating conditions as near to the womb as possible, give the baby the very best chance. Tiny babies receive supplements to help develop their lungs and now that more is understood about giving oxygen in incubators there is less chance of the eyesight damage that used to be a significant risk for these babies. So research is making delivery and infancy safer than ever for mothers and tiny babies. Sadly, some babies cannot survive or are left with disabilities or learning difficulties. A healthy, happy baby is a wonderful gift.

Chapter 2

Two key developmental processes – attachment and communication

Brain development, particularly in the early years

Figure 2.1 As Lilly and her mum enjoy their play they are developing the process of bonding and communication

Once babies are safely home, most parents are anxious to know the signs that show their offspring are making sound progress in all aspects of their development. New parents can find this an awesome responsibility and sometimes they are reluctant to ask questions in case they are thought not to be coping. Professionals who have been in touch with the family or who are taking full responsibility for day care from three months on or even earlier are also asking questions, so this chapter seeks to give answers, while reminding parents, carers and professionals that their seemingly fragile infants are usually quite robust. The chapter explains how babies' brains develop, allowing them to do more things, and it shares information about timetables for development. These can be used for guidance but the norms are wide; there may be differences across cultures and, in the main, babies will develop according to their innate timetable, i.e. in their own time. Learning to walk is a case in point. Some will walk at seven months; others wait until they are 20 months or so, and both are perfectly all right. Babies simply can't walk until they have the neurological development, the strength, co-ordination and balance that underlie this complex skill. Then they enjoy showing it off. Moreover, slow walkers may be very early talkers. They have been sitting absorbing the events around them, and unless there is a neurological difficulty, they *will* walk. Trying to rush them causes stress, so gentle encouragement, patience and lots of loving communication is best.

Let's listen to some questions posed by parents, carers and professionals now.

Q: What is the new baby able to do?

A: Although at birth human babies are the most dependent on the planet, they are far from helpless and new research techniques are discovering they have even more abilities than previously thought. Previously, paediatricians had to base their assessments solely on observations of the babies' appearance, e.g. were they a healthy pink colour or was there a blue tinge showing that their circulation might be causing problems? Were they alert or drowsy? Did they cry lustily or weakly because this could show how well their lungs were functioning? Were they well muscled or floppy, because this might mean that their **cerebellum** (the area at the back of the brain that controls muscle tone) was not functioning well? Were they able to clutch a finger and how soon were they able to support their heads and how did they respond to a stimulus? All of these observations were to check their alertness and movement strength.

These competences are still vitally important, and at birth the **Apgar score** is used to assess well-being. Babies are given a score (see Table 2.1) and assessed again ten minutes later when any birth trauma should have subsided. If the score is between seven and ten, paediatricians assume that the baby is doing well at this stage. Some suggest that the parents take a chart home and keep recording a score just to reassure everyone that the baby's well-being is sustained. It is important to note that movement occurs in each criterion – for circulation and breathing, even the heartbeat itself depends on movement.

Table 2.1 The Apgar score

Apgar score	Score 0	Score 1	Score 2
Heart rate	Absent	<100/min	>100/min
Respiratory rate	Not breathing	Weak cry: shallow breathing	Good strong cry: regular breathing
Muscle tone	Flaccid	Some flexion	Strong flexion and extension
Colour	Blue: pallid appearance	Body pink: feet blue	All pink
Response to a stimulus	None	Some limited response	Jerks; cries out. Reacts strongly

Paediatricians and researchers studying neonatal development also monitor babies' facial expressions as they encounter new tastes and their reactions as they hear different levels of sound, and they measure the babies' 'length of gaze' to see which patterns hold the babies' interest longest. As a result, they are able to claim that babies prefer complex patterns, such as their mother's face. Could this be an innate ability that promotes early bonding? Concerns resulting from any of these assessments could indicate difficulties but might not really pinpoint what was wrong.

Today, more sophisticated techniques such as magnetic resonance imaging (MRI) can actually look inside the brain. This allows researchers to find *how* the brain responds, or fails to do so. The invention of X-rays made a huge contribution to medical science when they allowed doctors to see inside the body to study bones and identify fractures. Now scans allow them to see the workings of the brain, so they can discover what is amiss or different when development doesn't proceed as expected, or when traumas such as cerebral palsy or epilepsy or even dyslexia affect the usual functioning of the brain.

Another technique, **Positron Emission Topography (PET)** identifies the brain areas that are working hardest by measuring their fuel intake (Carter 2000: 26). This promotes understanding of the best ways to intervene. One possible cause of dyslexia has been identified by PET scans that showed 'that the language processing areas failed to work in concert' (Carter 2000: 254) resulting in incoming words getting jumbled up and disjointed. At the very least these findings scotched the doubters' claims that the condition dyslexia did not exist and at best it pinpointed the most appropriate intervention. These techniques are expensive, however, and PET scanning is invasive in that it requires a radioactive marker to be injected into the bloodstream. Therefore, they are only considered if there is a significant medical reason for using them. The findings also need to be interpreted by experts in the field; nevertheless, the emergence of such techniques to discover developmental anomalies is a huge step forward.

Research is providing more sophisticated techniques to foster our understanding of babies' development and these studies point the way to finding the best interventions to reduce any difficulties. What do other parents and practitioners want to know about the newborn child?

Cara is anticipating the huge emotional impact that heralds the first sight of her baby and the joy in building a wonderful, lifelong relationship. No doubt she is worrying about coping with the baby too, so she is thinking ahead to practical issues such as getting help and support from the family. But once she has established that her baby is all right in that all the fingers and toes are there, she is concerned about the baby's emotional development. She asked the following question.

Q: How soon will my baby know that I am her mother? Does it matter if other family members look after her for a bit?

A: Cara will be pleased to hear that even newborn babies can distinguish their mothers from others by their smell and this gives them both comfort and security. There is a lovely Scottish expression that describes the baby nestling in the crook of its mother's arm – i.e. the baby 'coories in'. This suggests that a very special bond is developing. This is so important, for there is a basic psychoanalytic hypothesis that the quality of the child's earliest relationships affect the whole course of later developments (Sroufe *et al.* 1993). Many studies have shown that securely attached infants are later more capable at making friends and being more socially skilful through their lives. So it is truly worthwhile if mother and baby spend quality time together and do not let the rush of modern living spoil it.

The sense of touch (stimulated in 'coorie-ing in') is very important in establishing a bond. In newborns, this sense is more acute than either sight or hearing. Brain scans of touch-deprived children, e.g. Romanian orphans, reveal that areas of their brains are underactive. I wonder if understanding the importance of touch stimulated the use of baby massage as a key bonding and stress-releasing activity? I'm sure it did.

Cara also asks if it matters whether family members take a turn at looking after her baby. Having support can be vital, especially if the baby is irritable or constantly awake. If a mother knows that she can look forward to a break, then she will be less anxious and tired, states that do not facilitate bonding. Sometimes, however, new mothers can have too much conflicting advice about feeding times, sleeping times and baby routines and, having gratefully accepted experienced help in the first days, it can be difficult to establish their own preferred way. It is also important that babies develop relationships with other people, for they will provide other experiences for the baby. They might even help with the daily tasks that can seem overwhelming to new parents seriously deprived of sleep.

Babies' developing perceptual and social abilities are preparing them for the very important early interactions that facilitate the process of bonding and attachment. New parents will be watching their babies closely to wonder at these tiny beings, but they mustn't be disappointed that there aren't too many real smiles in the first few weeks, for when they do come, these communications make all the waiting worthwhile. Smiles win reciprocal smiles and hugs, so they encourage long-lasting positive relationships.

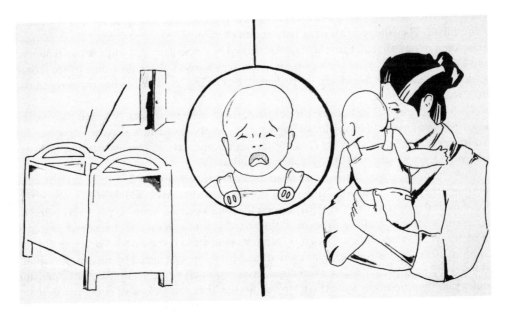

Figure 2.2 What should I do? Drawing by David Barrington.

Even before the time when babies can charm (control?) their families by smiling, their help-lessness means they have to entice someone into the care-giving role. Most do this superbly well by using different sounds and silences; in fact, many mothers will tell how the household revolves around interpreting and responding to their baby's cries or reacting to frightening periods of quiet. Mothers even have a hormonal surge that makes it virtually impossible for them to ignore a crying baby, and this can cause them to be constantly on the go.

Q: Babies have different types of cries, don't they? How can parents and carers tell if there is something wrong or if their babies just want even more attention?

A: It often takes a little experience for parents and carers to recognise the reasons for their babies' crying, to tell if there is really something wrong or if the baby is simply exercising its lungs. Crying is a very powerful means of expressing need and summoning support. One-month-old babies can communicate hunger, discomfort and fear by the different sounds they make, and they don't seem to care if their mothers have just sat down.

Q: How should parents and carers react to crying?

A: Parents often want to know if an immediate response makes babies secure and therefore placid and content, or if 'predictable responding', i.e. the baby knowing that their cries will bring someone running, will make them cry more. Hubbard and Van Ijzendoon (1997) offer some advice. They suggest that if the baby is signalling intense distress due to pain or hunger or needing to be changed, then the response should be immediate. But when babies whimper and listen, as when they are put down for a nap, they advise waiting for a time to see if they settle. The researchers found that immediately responding to milder crying encouraged the baby to cry even more.

The basic cry signalling hunger, they explain, tends to be rhythmical, whereas the one for anger is more intense. The cry indicating pain begins abruptly and is sharper. However, all babies develop their own ways of communicating through crying. Parents just have to listen and make a judgement, which is not an easy thing to do

Unfortunately, many babies suffer from colic, particularly in the first three months and although they won't remember the stress of that, their parents certainly will. Colic is the name for intense bouts of crying that happen for three or more hours per day, very often in the evenings, just when the parents need time to relax, or catch up and chat about concerns of their own. Babies can be agonised by tummy cramps and it can be hard or impossible to comfort them. At this time too, inexperienced parents are exhausted by their new respon-sibilities and perhaps they become frustrated, even depressed by feeling inadequate or perhaps guilty that they are doing something wrong. So this time can be one of stress and despair. Colic typically appears at about two weeks of age and lasts until three months. This is not good news for anyone, but this painful condition does go away.

One young mother whose baby cried and cried explained:

I just wanted her to love me, but she screamed and screamed and I could do nothing to quieten her. The neighbours were complaining; I had no money to go out and when I could bear it no longer, I just snapped and hit her. So she yelled some more. The social told me she had colic but I knew that. That was no help at all. I was so ashamed but I just wanted someone to take her away for a spell so that I could have a sleep. For even when I did doze off with her in the flat, I kept waiting for her starting to scream again. I wanted so much to be a good mum because I've never been good at anything else, but I've failed at that too. I'm desperate.

This scenario describes a terrible plight. How can mother and baby bond? Will long-term relationships be spoiled for good? Luckily, bonding and attachment is a process (Robinson 2011), not a one-off event. It need not be immediate. There is time for relationships to gel. Parents who have had to be separated from their newborns for medical reasons are assured of this. And even when there is no such difficulty, blips should be kept in proportion provided the baby was not hurt. Extra compensatory hugs and songs are better comforts than feelings of guilt. Beyond that, however, mothers who recognise that attachment isn't happening need support. We ignore such cries for help at our peril, yet immediate and continuing care support seems sparse.

Q: Can babies' cries do more than tell that they are hungry or upset? Can the sounds alert adults to the quality of their intellectual functioning?

A:Research findings (Huntington *et al.* 1990) show that some babies who experienced difficulties at birth, who were significantly early or who had other difficulties, e.g. tremors or fits, have a more piercing, grating cry. Researchers are beginning to agree that the quality of the baby's cry is significantly correlated to IQ and other cognitive measures at age two. So continual strident cries could be a communication that something beyond inexperienced parenting or under- or over-feeding needs investigation.

Q: Professionals, parents and carers are always fascinated by understanding babies' intellectual development. They can see and applaud the physical changes evident when the baby grows and is able to do more things, but understanding babies' intellectual development is a complex task. They ask, 'Are babies' brains just smaller, underdeveloped versions of our own? Are they fully developed at birth?'

A: The months just after birth are critical for optimum brain development. The new baby needs stimulation and communication as well as periods of rest, even though their brains keep working as they sleep. The text will give a brief introduction to the structure and function of the brain. A full explanation can be found in Carter (2000).

The brain

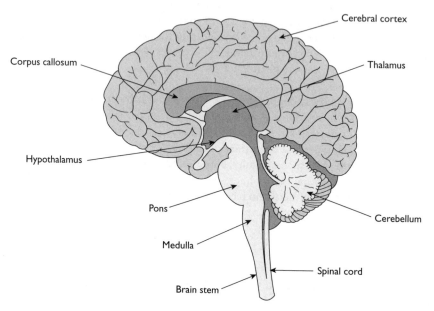

Figure 2.3 The brain

The brain has many different parts that work together to control our behaviour, to allow thinking and moving, remembering and transferring learning from one context to another.

At birth, the relatively helpless newborn is dependent on the brain stem. This is the most active area at this time because there are only a few connections to the cerebral cortex. It is part of the central nervous system and responsible for the neurons that control breathing, blood pressure and the general level of alertness, so is very important for survival. Parents and carers are always reminded to support the baby's head, not only because it is very heavy for the baby (it is proportionately twice the size and weight of an adult's head), but also to prevent any sudden shocks that could harm the brain stem. Any accident to the very core of the brain stem results in death. This protection continues through life. At the scene of any accident, for example, the paramedics will immediately stabilise this area with a neck brace to protect these vital functions.

The brain stem also holds the nerve tracts between the brain and the body, and this is where they cross from one side to the other. It also contains the pons and the **medulla oblongata**. This lower part of the brain is often called the reptilian brain because it is common to all vertebrates, from reptiles to man.

Linked to the brain stem is the reticular activating system (RAS), a complex bundle of **nerve fibres** that monitor sensory signals, causing them to stimulate or calm the sensations in different situations. It is vital in maintaining consciousness and arousal.

The **limbic system** is made up of different areas, e.g. the **amygdala** (the seat of mainly negative emotions), the hypothalamus (regulates hormones and helps control food intake and heart rate), the **hippocampus** (involved with **memory** and learning) and part of the **thalamus** (a relay station between the cortex and the sensory organs). They are all associated with learning, memory and emotional processing. The limbic system also holds the instincts, appetites and drives (motivation) that help us to survive (Winston 2004). Interestingly, it has been shown that the number of memory cells is markedly increased in those who are physically active. Activity also releases **endomorphins** into the bloodstream and also increases the flow of oxygenated blood around the body and the brain. This is why an early activity session each morning helps children concentrate later in the day.

The function of the amygdala is particularly interesting for research into autism. First, it is shaped differently (Moore 2004) and possibly because of this it biases the children's observations of events. Thus, the autistic child urged to recall a motor accident would speak about the red car or the flashing lights but not be perturbed by or even aware of the personal details such as the pain of the victim or the distress of the onlookers. The amygdala, which responds to negative emotions, also assigns a label to an object, e.g. 'this is good or bad'. Disorders in the amygdala and its association with the neurotransmitter dopamine may cause the recipient to see more things as bad or threatening and become phobic or depressed.

The midbrain forms a bridge connecting the lower structures to the cerebral cortex. It contains the **hypothalamus**, the basal ganglia and the thalamus, and these centres, with the cerebellum, organise the motor, sensory and autonomic systems. They are important centres for the planning and timing of actions.

Also working early at the back of the brain is the cerebellum. This area is sometimes known as the little brain because, like the cerebral cortex, it has two halves. It has a vital function in that it controls muscle tone. The quality of the muscle tone is assessed as part of the **Apgar score** for newborns (see Table 2.1). Later, as the baby becomes more independent, muscle tone is needed for balance, for co-ordinated movement and for control (more detail is given in Chapter 3). Claims as to what the cerebellum actually does are currently being rescrutinised, for new research indicates that there appears to be a language area situated there as well as at Broca's centre, which is responsible for language production, and Wernicke's centre, which deals with comprehension. These are both situated in the frontal cortex of the brain. This finding may help to explain the co-occurrence or, in medical terms, the co-morbidity between dyslexia and dyspraxia.

Although it can't initiate movement on its own, the cerebellum monitors all the impulses from the motor centres in the brain and from the nerve endings or **proprioceptors** in the muscles. It co-ordinates all the input from the senses, thus controlling every movement. Information from the vestibular sense (balance), from the eyes and from the lower limbs and trunk, all pass through the cerebellum. The cerebellum is also responsible for muscle tone. This is why activity strengthens the body.

Incoming information from all the senses is vast and the cerebellum sifts out the relevant information and passes it to the correct location for analysis. There are strong links with the frontal cortex (the part of the brain that deals with problem solving). New research is finding that the cerebellum is more involved with skill development, e.g. reading, than was previously thought, but of course reading is a motor skill. Links with memorising are also established. Damage to the cerebellum can cause paralysis in affected regions of the body and dysfunction can cause visual motor performance difficulties such as dyspraxia and dyslexia. In babies, the effects of poor cerebellar function can be seen when muscle tone is poor, i.e. when babies continue to be floppy past the time when they should have strengthened up and when all the motor milestones are delayed. Another sign in older children is when their gait is awkward and strange, e.g. in sustaining a wide leg stance or a side-to-side action with stiff knees beyond the time when this should have been overtaken by a forward, smooth heel–toe propulsion.

The cerebral cortex area at the top of the brain pyramid, or **cerebrum**, is composed of two hemispheres covered by a thin skin of deeply wrinkled grey tissue. The hemispheres are linked by the **corpus collosum**. Most tasks involve both hemispheres, although each has specialist functions. The right hemisphere has long been associated with creative thinking and artistry, but it is also involved in learning new tasks. Goddard (1996) explains that this area is a practice ground before the information goes through the corpus collosum to be refined. The left side is intimately concerned with language and organisation. Each hemisphere is split into four lobes. At the back, the occipital lobe is mainly made up of the visual processing area. The parietal lobe copes with movement, orientation and recognition, and the temporal lobe deals with sound, speech comprehension and memory. The **frontal lobes** deal with 'executive thinking', problem solving, conceptualisation and planning.

The corpus collosum, a thick band of fibres, transmits impulses from one hemisphere to the other. Its size is important because that controls the ease of transmission. Generally, in women it tends to be larger, which explains why they can multitask while men tend to focus on one thing at a time. The observation that the corpus collosum is smaller in boys has led to the idea that this is one reason why boys feature more in the numbers of children with special needs. On the other hand, the corpus collosum in gifted and talented children is large.

There are some significant structural differences in babies' brains that affect their function. The cells that actually create brain activity are **neurons**. By the time children are born, their brains contain about 100 billion neurons, but they are not mature. The information that comes from the senses is received by the **dendrites** and is passed along the **axon**, over the

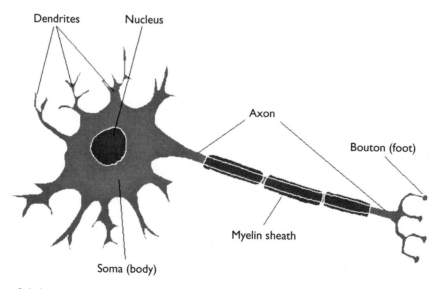

Figure 2.4 A neuron

synapse to the receiving dendrites of the next cell. In babies, most of the axons that transmit information have not yet grown, so the information does not pass from one to the next. And where this does happen, the axons are not yet myelinated.

Q: What does myelinated mean?

A: **Glial cells** form the support structures for the neurons. They have different functions. Some protect the neurons from undesirable toxins; some surround and ingest dead neuronal tissue and others form **myelin**, a fatty sheath that surrounds the axons and acts as an insulating fibre aiding the efficient and quick transmission of impulses along the axon. This myelin may not build up fully in all children until they are six, or even in some boys until adolescence.

PET scans show that in newborn brains, only the **brain stem**, the thalamus and the cerebellum are active. The other areas need time to mature.

Q: When will that happen?

A: Winston (2004: 247) explains that 'although the two year old brain is similar in shape and weight to an adult brain, specific areas such as the reward centre in the frontal cortex take years to develop and settle, growing, shrinking back and growing again'. This finding stimulated his research into delayed gratification in his television programme *Child of Our Time*. To test the hypothesis that children were impulsive and could not wait even when the delayed reward was better than the immediate one, he asked young children to delay eating a sweet placed in front of them on the promise of two sweets later on. A considerable number could not wait. He also explains that the part involved in paying attention only becomes fully developed at puberty. So the full function of the brain needs time to mature and this maturation corresponds to the rapid development that happens in the first formative and still dependent years.

In infancy, there are two major phases of brain development. At two or three months of age there is a rapid development of synaptic connections. These are 'experience–expectant' synapses that are preparing the brain to receive new experiences. The second phase, at two-plus years, is the development of 'experience-dependent synapses'. These are dependent on environmental experiences in order to be activated. The experiences stimulate the synapses so they firm up and survive. Unused synapses are pruned through the process of cell death and are ingested by the glial cells. This is known as 'pruning of the dendritic arbour'. The phrase 'use it or lose it' springs to mind.

Throughout the first year the connections between neurons firms up, making many more behaviours (resulting from decision making rather than spontaneous moves) possible. Brain activity increases in the parietal, temporal and visual cortices, and this is shown in the babies' growing awareness and reasoning about things in their environment. One of the early indicators of cognitive growth is babies' understanding of **permanence**, i.e. an object will still be there if it is covered by a cloth and out of sight. Babies involved in such experiments come to realise that, even when unseen, the object does not disappear. Professor Peter Willatt, then at Dundee University, found that babies could only plan and sequence an action based on this learning once the prefrontal cortex had reached a certain level of maturity and this, he found, happened between nine and ten months.

Before four years, the brain is not fully myelinated and the neurons respond by firming up patterns of connections. This endorses the value of early years education. It has also been proved that playing the piano and singing are superior to computer lessons in developing children's abstract reasoning skills, showing that even in the earliest years, particular experiences have a long-lasting effect on development. But why should fine motor skills such as playing an instrument have such an effect? Winkley (2004) explains that the tissue on each fingertip is connected to a large area in the frontal cortex and that pressure caused by playing an instrument or beating out rhythms stimulates this, and sets up activity and the formation of neural connections in this thinking part of the brain.

The peripheral and central nervous system

The whole surface of the body is connected to the brain through the central nervous system with a kind of mapping. The skin, muscles and joints are covered by proprioceptors or nerve endings, which are sensory receptors (the **peripheral nervous system**) that pass messages to the spinal column (the central nervous system) and then to the cortex. Each finger, as just one example, has its own cluster of neurons on the cortex, so children who use their fingers to count or to play a musical instrument, or even to act out rhymes such as 'Incy Wincy spider' are stimulating the cerebral cortex, the thinking part of the brain. Experiences help the brain make patterns of connections so that useful neural pathways are established.

The optic nerves in the eyes connect to the occipital lobe or visual areas of the brain for processing, while the vestibular sense (the sense of balance) connects to all the areas concerned to **neurotransmitters** initiate and control movement.

The **cerebro-spinal fluid**, a watery fluid made of **proteins** and glucose, surrounds and protects the brain and spinal cord. It is derived from the bloodstream and is filtered by ventricles in the brain.

There are many neurotransmitters but the most interesting in connection with children's learning are:

- Glutamate: a general-purpose neurotransmitter that acts to keep the passage of stimuli smooth and controlled.
- **GABA**: the most important inhibiting neurotransmitter. It prevents the brain being overloaded when too many neurons fire at once. If there is insufficient GABA, the system reacts chaotically, perhaps by fitting. GABA may deteriorate in old age.
- Dopamine: associated with voluntary action. Children who do not have enough dopamine have difficulty initiating and sustaining controlled movements. Variation in dopamine secretion is apparent in Parkinson's disease, in ADHD and other disorders. Dopamine is also linked to alcoholism, criminality and drug taking. Some genes will prevent dopamine binding to the neurons in the reward-motivating pathways of the brain, so those affected lack a feeling of satisfaction and are driven to seek more rewards, e.g. in gambling.
- Serotonin: the amount of serotonin influences the feel-good factor or mood of the child

or adult, and this can influence how others act towards him as well as how he tackles new learning. The level of serotonin may affect children's motivation. In depression, drugs are given to prevent the reabsorbtion of serotonin into the axon so losing its effect.

- Adrenaline: this is often felt in the body as tingling of the fingers in reaction to a startle or shock; the face reddens and the blood pressure rises. This is usually associated with a state of high alertness. Adrenaline should protect the body then subside.
- Noradrenalin acts in the brain to help us focus and pay attention.

So, if there is a lack of any neurotransmitter, any imbalance in production, or any inefficient transmission, then learning, movement and behaviour are all affected.

Q: In our setting we find that our youngest children are more inclined to be heartbroken at one moment and smiling again at the next. Why is that?

A: Young children are more instantly emotional than adults because the transmission of signals from the cerebral cortex (the convoluted area of neurons that enables us to perform complex tasks – see diagram on p. 28) is relatively weak. Some children cannot control outbursts because the axons or pathways that carry signals from the cortex to the limbic system (the area that is responsible for emotional control) have yet to grow. Yet the amygdala (the home of negative emotions such as anger or fear) is working well from birth. This means that the young brain is unbalanced, the amygdala being much stronger than the signals from the cortex. However, with calm role models and explanations, children can learn self-control. Early attempts to do this are likely to activate the cortex, thus stimulating the growth of the axons. Children who give their tantrums free rein (and parents who pay attention to them and so reinforce their behaviour) are letting their amygdala win. Anger allows **cortisol** to flood the frontal cortex and the centres for logical thought and reasoning become overwhelmed and are put out of action. So these poor behaviours are often caused by immaturity.

It is interesting to find that Carter (2000: 19), has discovered that 'a baby's brain contains some things an adult's does not'. She explains that there are connections between the auditory (hearing) and visual (seeing) cortices, and others between the retinas in the eyes and the part of the thalamus that takes in sound, so babies may see sounds and hear colours. Sometimes, this way of perceiving is retained in adults and is called synaesthesia. It is fascinating to know that babies have skills that adults have lost. Swimming is another example, for all newborns can swim. They instinctively kick to propel themselves through water. This may be a left-over skill from when they were immersed in the amniotic fluid in the womb. Babies can even feed underwater as the passageway to the lungs cuts off to prevent them from drowning. They have an inbuilt walking reflex, too. At six days, if someone supports their weight, they will make stepping motions, passing one foot then the other in a bipedal action. However, like the ability to swim, this disappears shortly after birth.

Q: So babies have some reflex movements that disappear. Why is this? If the environment was right in terms of providing opportunities, could these be retained?

A: Let's answer the second part of that question first. In the 1980s, researchers at a College of Physical Education carried out a pilot study to try to find if new babies could retain their early swimming ability if they had daily swimming sessions. Their mothers or carers took them into the pool without any artificial support. While most babies enjoyed the water and appeared to gain confidence – a valuable outcome in itself – none of the group of about 20 babies retained the ability to swim. Unfortunately, the chlorine in the water affected the skin of one or two of the babies, so the experiment was curtailed earlier than anticipated but the researchers (Macintyre and Murdoch: 1986) considered they had enough data to make tentative conclusions that the early swimming abilities were not retained.

Babies' motor skills are not well developed and as parents tend to observe and perhaps make general assessments from their motor skills, e.g. their inability to move from the spot or their apparently aimless and unco-ordinated reaching and stretching actions, they may be misled into believing that babies are less able than is actually the case. Babies do practise a limited range of skills, e.g. waving and kicking, but they are unco-ordinated and purposeless at this stage. Carefully detailed observations by researchers such as Thelen (1981) observed that kicking movements peak just before a baby crawls. Perhaps the rhythmical movements strengthen the babies' legs ready for the weight bearing and propulsion that crawling requires. Another fascinating finding is that a sense of safety develops two weeks after babies learn to crawl. The two weeks in between must be hazardous indeed.

Adaptive and primitive reflexes

Q: I've heard that babies are born with a cluster of reflexes. I've heard of the Moro and the Babinski reflexes. Are these automatic physical responses to specific stimuli such as the knee jerk in adults responding to the tap below the knee?

A: The new baby has a set of adaptive reflexes that help him survive, e.g. the sucking, swallowing and rooting reflexes. In the latter, a touch on the baby's cheek causes turning to that side to feed. These should not be present in older children; they simply help the newborn to sustain life. Some reflexes do remain even though they are no longer required, e.g. stroking the palm of baby's hands will cause strong closure of the fingers. This is not useful for the babies themselves, although parents often enjoy the feel of baby holding on tightly, recognising this as a sign of strength and communication.

Some adaptive reflexes do persist through life, e.g. quickly withdrawing a hand from an object that is too hot, so ensuring safety. Some are less visible, e.g. the pupil of an eye adjusting to different levels of light and goose bumps developing to help cope with the cold.

Primitive reflexes are so called because they are controlled by the primitive part of the brain. If babies are startled by a loud noise or by a sudden jab, the Moro reflex causes them to arch their backs and throw their hands wide in an attempt to get away from the source of distress. This has been functioning before birth, and at birth if the baby does not breathe, the midwife will induce the reflex, causing the baby to throw the head back, extend the chest wall and breathe in. Once the baby is safely breathing this is no longer necessary and during the first few weeks it should be washed away. In fact, retaining this reflex, which is often called the 'fight or flight' reflex, can cause children to withdraw or to be in a state of alarm or stress, ready to escape the scene or to lash out aggressively as a survival mechanism. Children who are anxious or who have anxiety-linked allergies may have a retained Moro reflex.

However, some features of the Moro reflex still have uses. The arousal system plays a big part in this response. If, for example, you hear a loud bang when everything should be quiet or if there is no noise when there should be sound, then the auditory signal or lack of it alerts the amygdala to trigger fear. Thereafter, the hypothalamus calms all activity to allow thought and preparation. It then swings into reverse so that blood pressure rises and breathing rates increase so that the body is primed for fight or flight. Mothers who are alarmed by their babies' sound sleeping with shallow breathing will recognise this instinctive cycle of events.

There is a whole group of primitive reflexes that should be washed away by about six months of age, and when they disappear, more sophisticated postural reflexes take their place. This can happen when the parts of the brain that control movement and perception, thinking and language have reached that stage of development. In fact, retained primitive reflexes can indicate neurological delay. They may hinder further learning. Parents and teachers are often surprised when bright, articulate children have severe writing difficulties. This may be due to a retained reflex and at therapy children are encouraged to revisit the earlier patterns of development such as crawling 'to give the brain a second chance' (Goddard 1996: 3). The aim is to jettison reflexes that should not be there. The study of reflexes is beyond the scope of this text, but interested readers may want to read any of Sally Goddard Blythe's work (see the References).

Is breast-feeding best?

Q: Can the baby's diet have any impact on this cognitive growth? Mothers, carers and professionals were all particularly interested in this question. The latter group explained that they were often asked to give advice. Is breast still best?

A: Despite all the progress in making formula milks, it seems that breast is still best in terms of what it can do for both mother and child. First, being held close becomes associated with pleasant feeding sensations and helps bonding, although bottle-feeding can achieve this too. And as 'feeding distance' is the best visual distance for new babies, the relationship can be built on eye contact as well as through touch, taste and smell. Mothers who cannot feed their babies have a very good substitute in formula milk. Bottle-feeding also allows the father to have a turn and share the pleasure.

The composition of breast milk is better, however, for it helps ward off infections. Breast milk contains immunoglobulins that provide a lining to the stomach and immunoproteins that act against disease and also as a food supplement. Breast milk also has a higher fatty acid content, making it healthier and promoting the growth of nerves and the intestinal tract. For mothers who find breast-feeding logistically impossible, knowing that even one breast feed per day brings benefits for the baby can be a comfort. This can happen at night when the day's activities are over.

The other part of the question asked about the relationship with cognitive development. This is hard to prove because of the huge number of intervening variables that need to be controlled, but healthier babies are usually happier babies and this helps relationships to gel. As the benefits are claimed to last beyond early childhood, at the very least the children will have fewer days off school. So there may well be an indirect correlation between breast feeding and cognitive success.

In the poorest countries of the world women have been persuaded that formula milk is as good as or even better than breast milk, with few instructions about sterilisation even when flies are rampant. Some mothers even had to water down the formula to make it go further. Perhaps the quality of the water was suspect or maybe sterilisation was not adequate, but certainly bottle-fed babies in underdeveloped countries are far more susceptible to dying from diarrhoea. They lack the antibodies that could have been supplied by breast milk.

Q: You mentioned benefits to the mother. I had never heard of these, or at least beyond the idea of building a relationship. What are they?

A: The benefits are significant, for breast feeding reduces the risk of osteoporosis (by prolactin increasing the uptake of calcium in the diet) and its hormonal effects may even help counteract the potential cancer-causing properties of **oestrogen** and progesterone. Breast-feeding also helps the uterus shrink back to its pre-pregnancy size. So there are many reasons why breast is best.

Q: There is so much to learn and viewpoints are ever changing. How are we to cope?

A: By reading, thinking and trying to do the best you can. Luckily, most babies are robust but all benefit from their parents and carers knowing the best way to comfort, to console and to stimulate the children so that they develop trust and respect as they set out on the long learning pathway.

Chapter 3

The growing child
From toddlerhood to three years

As children become toddlers they grow and mature, and so become capable of many more things. This is a time when children get much joy from their achievements and this can be seen when they repeat and practise activities that have pleased them. It is fascinating to see how the changing competences are reflected in the different aspects of their development, i.e. in play, movement and language (see Table 3.1).

The innate process of maturation supported by the quality of the interactions and environments they have experienced allows young children to become independent learners

Table 3.1 Changes in development

Play	Language	Movement
5 years		
Can initiate or join in role play,	Can follow/retell a story without pictures. Can read simple words. Can tell a short imaginative story.	Can run and jump, ride a bike and zip a coat. Understands the rules of major games.
4 years		
Understands pretence and develops fears of the unknown. Develops imaginative games, not always able to explain rules.	Knows colours and numbers. Can explain events, hopes and disappointments. Able to listen and focus.	Can climb and swing on large apparatus. Has a developed sense of safety outdoors. Can swim. Enjoys bunny jumps and balancing activities.
3 years		
Enjoys group activities, e.g. baking a cake for someone's birthday. Understands turn taking.	Uses complex sentences. Understands directional words and simple comparisons, e.g. big/small.	Can ride a trike and climb stairs. Climbs in and out of cars/buses independently. Can catch a large ball.
2½ years		
Develops altruism, especially for family members. Understands emotional words, e.g. happy, sad.	Uses pronouns and past tenses adding 'ed' to form own version of past tense.	Uses a step-together pattern to climb stairs. Can walk some distance.

Table 3.1 continued

Play	Language	Movement
2 years		
Beginning to play alongside a friend for a short time (parallel play).	Rebels – says 'No.' Can form two-word sentences but comprehension is far ahead of speech.	Can walk well but jumping is still difficult. Climbs on furniture (check cross-lateral crawling pattern).
18 months		
Sensorimotor play exploring the properties of objects (solitary play).	Has ten naming words. Points to make wishes known.	Can crawl at speed and walk but jumping is not developed. Balance is precarious.
1 year		
Walks unsteadily, arms and step pattern wide to help balance.	Enjoys games, e.g. peek-a-boo. Beginning to enjoy books and stories. Monosyllabic babbling.	Plays with toys giving them correct usage – simple pretend, e.g. feeding doll.
6–8 months		
Can sit unsupported briefly. Rolls over from back to tummy. Attempts to crawl.	Makes sounds and blows bubbles.	Reaching out for objects now. Changing objects from one hand to the other.
0–4 months		
May be able to support head but weight of head makes this difficult. Strength developing head to toe and centre to periphery. Can lift head briefly in front lying.	Early communication: responds to voices: can make needs known by different cries.	Plays with hands as first toy. Can hold object placed in hand but cannot let go – object drops. Movements unco-ordinated.

and decision-makers, and increasingly they become social beings, ready to share and take turns, and become involved in someone else's game. This is an innate developmental sequence. Clearly, the children's physiological changes, i.e. greater strength, longer limbs and steadier movements, enable more exploration and encounters. Also, they are matched by psychological changes that impact on their development. These changes can be seen in the way three-year-olds behave at home and at school.

Carers, professionals and practitioners often have a larger input into children's lives nowadays, so let's find out what questions they wish to ask.

Q: I hear a lot about attachment theory. I know that to be securely attached is a good thing, but can this lead to problems when my child goes to nursery?

A: Let's take the first part first. An attachment or, in Ainsworth's (1972) terms, '**an affectational bond**' is 'a relatively long-enduring tie where there is a desire to maintain closeness'. Attachment behaviours are more easily observed in the early years because they are overt. Toddlers and young children are more needy than older ones because, rather like Andrew in the case study on p. 47, they have not experienced so many events and recognised that they will survive and be all right. So they will cry and cling or follow closely to show distress, whereas the older child will wave or gesture or touch to confirm his relationship. Having said that, even some five-year-olds can be really upset for a considerable time when they go to school and their parents can be surprised at this reaction. It may be that the strange environment is daunting because it is very busy and the child is overwhelmed, or it may be that well-meaning adults have painted a picture that does not match reality.

Such attachment depends on the opportunity parents have to develop **synchrony**, i.e. a complex pattern of interactions where trust builds up and where expectations are met. The strength of a child's attachment to their father in the early years can depend on the time he has available to be with them. One researcher actually counted the number of nappies a father changed as a means of measuring contact time, but surely that concentrated on quantity rather than quality?

Babies are about six months before real attachments are formed and at that time babies begin to use their parents as a safe base. This is apparent when the child crawls away but constantly looks back to check that their mother or father is still there. The ten-month-old toddlers show a new cognitive change when they begin to check out their mother's or father's

Figure 3.1 Lilly teaches her dad to play her game. She is taking the lead role, challenging her balance and developing her fine motor skills

expression before attempting a new venture. This is a big step forward in **social referencing** and is a lovely example of how the different aspects of development progress together.

Fear of strangers and separation anxiety appear at about 12–16 months. At that time children who have appeared secure can seem to regress to being clingy again and this stage can last until 24 months or so. This can be frustrating for parents who need to go back to work, but babies can't be rushed and this stage *will* pass.

By the time the children are two or three, their attachment behaviours become less visible (although the attachment itself is as strong). By this age children's **cognition** allows them to realise that their mother's promise that she will come back will be fulfilled, so this is a good time to contemplate sending them to nursery. Children will seek out proximity after a parent returns from being away for a spell – sometimes they will behave very badly for a while as if they wished to punish the parent for the absence, but in known places they are able to tolerate separation without distress. A strategy that is possible and helpful at this stage is for parents and children together to make plans, e.g. what the child will do if they feel upset or what they will do together when they go home.

Of course, parents can stay with their children for a while until the new nursery personnel and the play environment becomes familiar, and thereafter periods of separation can be gradually increased. In many, even most cases, mothers 'suffer' more than the children themselves.

> Q: I've heard that boys can dress up as girls at nursery and play with dolls. I'm not sure this is a good idea. Does this not just confuse the children's identity?

A: Children develop a very early and robust notion of gender (Fagot 1995). Even in families where boys and girls are treated the same with no rewarding for sex-type behaviour, e.g. in toy choice, play behaviour or choice of dress, they develop a strong **sense of gender**. This develops in three stages. The first is when the child notices the difference between males and females at about 18 months and when they gradually realise they are boys or girls. This is securely in place by about 2½ years. Bigler (1995) explains that this comes about because society is full of references to gender, e.g. 'Great you've got a boy – you'll be able to take him to football matches' or 'Wow, a girl – think of the pretty dresses you'll buy' or 'Is the new baby a boy or girl? I'll buy a pink/blue card.' In many homes toys may be separated subconsciously into boy and girl selections and this may lead to children playing in same-sex groups even though no one has suggested that they do so.

As early as two years, some children will imitate gender roles reinforced by videos and books that are given as presents. Bob the Builder and Angelina Ballerina are just two favourites. I don't think there is a Tomasina tank engine? The point is that children begin to associate certain behaviours with these symbols. It seems that even young children have strong sex stereotypes. The idea that mothers make cakes and if they work they are nurses or teachers, while fathers make money and are joiners or car salesmen persists, even though the evidence in the home may well tell them otherwise. Gradually, they learn gender constancy, i.e. that they will stay as a boy or a girl all of their lives unless they are very unhappy in the gender they have been given. Some children are unsure about this when they are four

Figure 3.2 Children are free to enjoy dressing up. They are not hampered by gender stereotyping

or five. Professor Robert Winston, in his famous TV series *Child of Our Tme*, asked a child who knew he was a boy, 'Will you be a man or a lady when you grow up?' The child looked bemused. Perhaps he was unsure or perhaps it was the strange question that caused him to frown. Perhaps he was thinking too much and trying to discover an underlying agenda. One can never tell – just be fascinated.

Some research shows that sex stereotypes are less pronounced in children who have been brought up by their fathers, but there is not enough research evidence to make claims that will stand scrutiny. Perhaps additional research needs to examine the biological development of 'feminine' boys and girls who exhibit more masculine traits. If this is down to hormones, then appearances may show the differences and indeed 'feminine boys' have often been found to be good-looking and gentle, and searched out by girls. Boys who play with dolls for a while may become loving fathers; girls who like tools and 'boys' activities' will be able to excel at DIY. Let's not limit our children by society's outdated **schema**.

The key point is that each child is a product of their nature and nurture. In my view, parents have to empower their children to be what they wish to be, for each has only one life. It may be short, it may be long, but it should be joyous. Parents must give their children roots, but also aim to give them wings.

> Q: When I get new three-year-olds into my setting, I often have to convince the parents and carers that their children will learn best through play. They are anxious that they learn to count to ten because they have read that is part of a new proposal for assessment for four-year-olds. When I tell them that rote learning is less useful than learning in a meaningful play context, they look sceptical. What should I do?

A: I think there are two ways forward. The first is to invite all the carers and parents into the setting to show them how involved the children are in their different activities. You could explain to them exactly what they are learning through play and how that links to formal learning later on (for a full explanation, see Macintyre (2011)). The second, especially for children who are newly three, is to share Susan Isaacs's quotation 'Play is the means by which children come to understand the world . . . they live in. . .' (Isaacs 1933). This, in my view, encapsulates the huge learning potential within play when children have the freedom to do what interests them at their own pace in a supported environment. Alternatively, you might share the list of characteristics of play, as follows:

- enjoyment in the activity;
- freedom to choose what to do and to make changes;
- decision making about what to do and how long to do it;
- time to follow a plan;
- no fear of failure;
- satisfaction in doing something or making something of your own;
- for the three- and four-year-olds, learning to play with someone else.

> Q: Do you think that would help?

A: I'm not sure, for some parents may see 'freedom' as wasting time, especially when the children don't set out to make something or learn a specific skill. They don't seem to appreciate the social learning that happens when they learn to share, to take turns and to be part of a group. When I explained that going for a walk involves observing the environment, learning how to look and marvelling at what they see, they were silenced but not convinced. When I explained that understanding how reflections were made was really science, that pleased them.

Figure 3.3 Understanding how reflections are made is an early science lesson

Q: Could you explain that you plan each part of the day and have a balance of activities so that there is time for the children to choose, but also they have a story with discussion time and at snack they learn about healthy eating as well as counting grapes and raisins? In fact, letting them see how children learn to set the table and explaining all the mathematical thinking that goes on there – things like one-to-one correspondence – might be a good way to quieten their concerns. What do you think?

A: I would take the parents into the outdoor area and show them where the children have planted seeds and learned about growing, made food balls for the birds and learned the different species that will visit us and learned about the mini-beasts that live in our old tree trunk. You are explaining the width of learning opportunities that really enhance their learning, but I wonder if you might explain, possibly later, what the children gain from fantasy play as well.

Q: How could we do that when sometimes we are not sure what the children are doing, far less learning?

A: Yes, this is difficult when the play ideas change as you watch. I think I'd talk about the affective side of the children's development, noting things like concentration, considering different ideas and plans, and selecting one, following it through – that sort of thing. And, of course, you can ask a child, 'Would you like to explain to us. . .?' but be prepared for the answer, 'No.' Parents might be upset by that response, but that in itself tells you the children have the confidence to assert their feelings. Hopefully, they will have said it politely.

You have also to be sure to explain that although the children are free to choose, you, as professionals, are not free. You have to observe and analyse, and record the children's progress and respond to all their different ploys.

Q: A linked way would be to show the parents our observation schedules to let them see how you monitor progress in a developmental area. Then they can be sure that their child has a balanced curriculum. How would that do?

A: I think that's wonderful. Of course, there's all the documentation such as the Early Years Foundation Stage (EYFS), the Early Years Professional Status (EYPS), and the Curriculum for Excellence that all support play as a key medium for learning. They also show the opportunities practitioners have to gain further qualifications. That surely shows that the early years curriculum has been the source of discussion and debate by experts in the field?

Q: Some parents and carers are overly concerned by safety. When I suggested that the children come in play clothes, they nearly freaked out. What would they be doing that spoiled their clothes, they asked?

A: It's hard for some parents and carers to accept that taking risks is part of growing up and becoming independent. Three-year-olds should enjoy climbing and swinging and balancing. Some can even handle hammers and saws with finesse, but you should explain that these activities are closely supervised and carefully chosen in line with each child's level of competence. Parents just have to accept that there might be minor scratches and bumps. This would fulfil the EYPS criterion 'Recognise when a child is at risk of harm and know how to protect them.' After all, they could be at risk at home. Another idea might be to show parents a care plan for children with allergies or other special needs, and then they can discover how their children learn to empathise and support less fortunate children without being patronising.

I think these opportunities to develop empathy in children are critically important. Adults setting out to encourage this 'should model awareness of how their own actions impact on others' (Robinson 2010). Even if you don't have real children with problems, you can role-play hospitals and/or cultural events that allow children to appreciate pictures of different realities.

Q: A picture of reality? What's that?

A: As the children experience these happenings, which may be familiar or strange, they are building an internal model of the world around them and at the same time developing a sense of self. This 'sense of self' is a part of the child's developing self-concept or the picture children build of themselves as they grow. Their self-esteem is the evaluative part of that picture and it may match or conflict with what others believe the child to be. The child's body image plays an important part too, and again the child's conception of himself may be far from what adults think it should be. While the self-concept is formed gradually in the process of growing up, the roots are laid down in the early formative years and once it has been formed it can be hard to shift.

Q: I wonder how you can change this picture? I have a child who is being fostered after being taken from her birth parent who was unable to cope. She is a lovely child and very bright but, despite these advantages, she has a very low self-esteem. She doesn't trust adults because so many promises have been broken, so my giving praise doesn't have much effect and she shies away from being touched. The picture she has of reality has been harsh and she is afraid that the better picture she is beginning to experience won't last. Her previous foster carers explained that she is socially very unsure and when she tries to make a friend she suffocates them and that makes them go off with someone else. She feels rejected again. So I'd be glad to hear about how the picture of reality is formed.

A: Epstein (1991) has analysed this picture. He claims that there are four important elements, which he suggests build to 'a picture of reality'. These are:

1   A belief about whether the world is about pleasure or pain.
2   A belief about whether the world is predictable and controllable, rather than chaotic and confusing.
3   A belief about whether people are desirable or threatening.
4   A belief about self-worth.

Reading these, it is obvious that these beliefs are based on the upbringing the children have experienced during their early years and that children who have experienced different levels of love and support will establish a more or less positive set of beliefs. For practitioners, such a list evokes much reflection on the ways different families rear their children. Parents will consider their own interaction skills possibly in terms of consistency and reliability, and possibly how they dealt with emotional events that have interrupted the tenor of their lives. Did they shield the children from turbulence or were they party to the disquiet? Carers and practitioners reading the list will be seeking to understand the source of the varying outlooks and attitudes of different parents and children in their care. Also, all the adults may well be wondering how the children from very different families will adapt when they meet up in a new setting and must learn to conform to new 'rules'.

The first 'belief' might make parents consider the balance of happy and sad episodes in their child's life and cause them to ponder on how both they and their child coped in sad times. This particularly brings to mind children who have many hospital visits and explains why hospitals do their best to cheer the atmosphere and disguise the unpleasant things that have to happen. A child's **temperament** plays a large part here because some little ones appear to be amazingly resilient, accepting their lot with equanimity and winning a great deal of admiration as they do. All children have to cope with sadness, perhaps at the death of a grandparent or pet, and parents can feel overwhelmed by not knowing what to do. Collins (2005) in *It's OK to be Sad* offers advice on ways for parents to comfort children through bereavements.

The second belief refers to whether routine or chaos is the child's lot. A set routine does allow children to anticipate what comes next and so contributes to security, but if this is too rigid the danger is that changes become things to be avoided, even feared. Many children nowadays have a rather rigid daily timetable of events with little freedom or opportunity to experience unforeseen changes in routine or to take risks or even to play. Perhaps this will make them obsessive about 'rules'. On the other hand, in a more laissez-faire approach, children can be fazed by unpredictability and not knowing what comes next, where they are to go and with whom. Whether these ad hoc experiences lead to fun and relaxation or to uncertainty and anomie will depend on the children's temperament, the role models the children see and to what extent they feel in control of the situation. How often these unexpected events happen will be important too, but again the children's **personality** in terms of introversion/extroversion plays a big part.

The third belief may also give parents pause for thought about the people who come into contact with their children. They need to appreciate their children's interpretation of what loud voices or trendy clothes or over-effusive manners means. It can be difficult for any child to relate to children or adults who do not match those they already know, but how much more alarming is this for those who find it difficult or impossible to read the facial expressions or the non-verbal communication of others? The vastly increasing number of children on the autistic spectrum will spring to mind here.

Case study

Andrew is a ten-year-old boy who has autism. At school he could manage his day provided there were no changes in routine but he was very afraid of men. One day at snack time a friendly young man, Sam, who was unaware of the dismay his presence caused, came to the table, sat near Andrew and was ready to join in passing the juice around. Andrew froze, then he screamed and tried to run from the table. The visitor was aghast that he had caused this and got up ready to leave, but the teacher said 'Please stay.' She explained that Andrew had to learn to tolerate experiences like this. He had to realise that he was safe in the company of men. She hoped that if he could just tolerate Sam for a while, he would realise he had survived and that he would store this in his memory to help him through the next encounter.

Understanding the difficulties many children have saves us taking 'normal developments' for granted.

Epstein's fourth belief is about self-worth. How are we to support our children's developing self-belief? Observing children closely and giving praise readily whenever it is due is a good way, especially so in the early years. Furthermore, when things aren't going well, trying to divert the children's attention rather than getting into a conflict situation is best, for confrontation tends to escalate, with no winners at the end. Another strategy is to avoid personal comments until you are sure they are in line with what the child wants. 'Aren't you big/small/clever/fat/thin?' can all be resented or misconstrued by children who would prefer not to be any of these things. Although a global sense of self-worth does not usually develop until about age six, the seeds are sown much earlier. A self-scheme and a gender-scheme begin to form at age two (Bee and Boyd 2005: 454). These authors endorse Epstein's claim that 'These four beliefs created in infancy are likely to be the most basic and therefore the most resistant to change at later ages.' The importance of the early years in formulating a positive belief system cannot be overstated.

Q: A parent with two children at nursery asks, 'It's quite confusing to hear that there are different models of parenting. We just do what comes naturally at the time, but perhaps if we understood more we would make different choices. Sometimes, after a scrap we try to reflect and we recognise that we are inconsistent with our son. At the supermarket, when he yells, we give in and let him have a lollipop to keep him quiet in the trolley, and now he knows this and behaves badly every time. We try to be firm but it's easier to give in. Let's be honest, we'd do anything for a bit of peace, but he's turning into a tyrant and ruling the roost. What should we be doing?

A: Maccoby and Martin (1983) proposed a model that has been very influential. They emphasised two dimensions, namely, the parents' degree of demand or control and their level of acceptance/responsiveness. These suggested four parenting types, as follows.

The **authoritarian** type: these parents have a set of standards and their children must comply. They are very demanding but have low levels of communication or responsiveness. They expect unquestioning obedience. They impose rules with no explanations or leeway. How does this affect the children? Some accept and tolerate them; some value such direction; some are subdued while others show levels of aggressiveness and rebellion. Interestingly, these children do less well in school. While they relish rote learning, they have not been involved in discussions about different viewpoints and so find it hard to recognise and respect another point of view. It is claimed that the out-of-control child is likely to come from this type of family, especially if the parents are authoritarian but do not have the skills to enforce the rules they set (Patterson 1996).

The second type is the *permissive* one when children have parents who are tolerant and warm but do not have much say over what their children do. As a result, the children have difficulty in accepting control in another setting and are less ready to become independent. They tend to be immature in their behaviour and avoid responsibility.

The **authoritative** type of parenting is the third type and produces the most positive outcomes in the children. The parents have high expectations and they readily offer praise and support in all circumstances. When expectations are not met, explanations rather than punishments are the order of the day, but these are firm so that borderlines are understood. Children are respected and their views are sought. In turn, they respect their parents. They tend to have a higher self-esteem than other children and thrive on and seek out responsibility.

The last type is the *neglecting* parent. Children brought up in this way are likely to have many negative outcomes. Parents may be depressed or ill and unable to provide security and care. There may be no bonding and little nurture, so the children feel no responsibility and reciprocate in kind. These children show disturbed behaviour and have problems with building relationships that last.

While these different categories are helpful for parents and for practitioners striving to understand why differences in children's behaviour and expectations occur, there are many 'is likely to' phrases because children do not come in one mould and several factors such as temperament, personality, even the place in the family all make a difference. Authoritative households can produce rebellious, unhelpful children and some who come from neglectful homes do surprisingly well. The statistics underlying the claims, however, come from pieces of research that gather data from thousands of homes to produce 'norms'. There will always be exceptions, however. Interestingly, the best outcome is when authoritative parents maintain relationships with the playgroup/nursery/school that adopts the same ethos, for then parents and professionals together can work together to secure the best outcome for each child.

Chapter 4

The importance of movement for enjoying living and learning

One of the most important things that parents, professionals and carers can do for babies, toddlers and young children is to observe and encourage the development of their movement patterns. This is because movement, as well as being very important in its own right, helps children to become confident learners in all aspects of their development – social, emotional and intellectual. This is why Goddard (1996: 5) writes:

> Movement is an integral part of life from conception until death and a child's experience of movement will play a pivotal role in shaping their personality, their feelings and achievements. Learning is not just about reading, writing and maths. These higher abilities are built on the integrity of the relationship between brain and body.

More and more researchers are finding that if the basic movement skills are mastered, the child has a solid foundation on which to build all the activities of daily living, at home, in any setting and at school.

Many parents may be surprised to hear that their child's ability to crawl using the cross-lateral pattern provides a key developmental milestone, even contributing to writing competence later on. Furthermore, most of the early observations about babies concern their movement skills – their breathing, their ability to support their heads; their strength in clutching a finger; when they sit unsupported and when they walk. When all of these happen 'at the right time' parents can be reassured that development is on track and that the other linked aspects of development are likely to be secure as well. When there is delay leading to concern, movement assessments are among the first that can be carried out, pinpointing what is wrong and providing the clues as to what intervention is needed. Such observations, however, need an understanding of how and when movement abilities develop, and enhancing babies' and toddlers' movements needs knowledge of a range of strategies and the perception to choose those that best suit the babies' age and stage of development.

These are quite sophisticated things to do, for babies are individuals with their own likes and dislikes, and their own innate timetables of development. Moreover, progress doesn't follow a smooth curve; it happens at different times, and in stops and starts. Some babies are constantly on the go, ready to experiment, while others are more contemplative and cautious in their approach. Personality and temperament are also part of the equation and this may make decisions about what to do next and how to go about it quite tricky. However, there are guidelines or charts to help reassure parents or provide evidence that

Figure 4.1 The cross-lateral pattern is more easily observed in climbing

there is delay that needs expert support. So, if babies are not attempting to do the movements described in the motor milestones table, at the 'right time', even though normative time is wide, advice from a GP or health visitor should be requested (see Table 4.1 on p. 58).

Babies bring 'a genetic blueprint' with them when they are born and, to some extent, this influences what they will choose to do and when they will do it. This is the nature side of their development. However, the opportunities parents and carers provide will build on this and support their children so much. This is the nurture side. Interacting with children and encouraging them appropriately doesn't need money or expensive resources – just time, patience and a clear understanding of the best ways to encourage progress.

This chapter sets out to provide guidance on key developmental competences in movement and strategies for parents, carers and practitioners to choose from. It also provides reasons why such activities will enhance the babies' development. Playing together should be fun. The questions in this chapter, as in the others, have been asked by a variety of parents, carers, practitioners and other professionals. The answers very often come from them, too, as they share ways they have found helpful for their children. The professionals bring knowledge from research and lengthy times in the field. It's also a good idea for everyone involved in observing the children to try the movements themselves. After all, it may be a long time since they tried crawling and they may be surprised how perplexing it can be, especially if they naturally would use a homolateral, one-sided pattern and have to think hard to adopt the cross-lateral one. Perhaps they were one of those children who didn't crawl, going straight from sitting to walking. Although that is entirely possible, many, even most children who didn't crawl, couldn't crawl using the cross-lateral pattern, i.e. one hand and the opposite knee going forward. A substantial number of non-crawlers or homolateral crawlers/bum shufflers will have difficulties with dexterity and crossing the midline. So difficulties in activities such as writing or using a knife and fork might have been prevented by regular early crawling practices using the cross lateral pattern. Bum shuffling and homolateral crawling, i.e. the hand and knee on the same side going forward together, do not provide the same benefits, although the children may go at speed and be reluctant to change. Those who teach crawling need to be able to do it – or at least understand the correct cross-lateral pattern before they teach children.

Think ahead to the time when children go to playgroup or nursery or children's centres. They want to be able to enjoy climbing on the frame, fastening up their coats independently, threading beads and doing what the other children do – movement should be fun.

If children can't catch a ball or paint a rainbow, their peers can see their unco-ordinated attempts. Movement is public and other children can be quick to tease. This hurts and is

Figure 4.2 Jordan is exhilarated by his skill. He practised and practised until he found the combination of rhythm and speed that allowed him to build a sequence of leaps

likely to affect the children's developing self-esteem, as movement is the foundation for many different kinds of learning – social (think of shaking hands or carrying plates or co-operating in a game of football), intellectual (think how action songs such as 'Five little buns in a baker's shop' help to memorise the words and the numbers) and emotional (think of the confidence that comes from being able to help another child to bake or pour water or even swim), as well as the motor one itself. Of course, moving well is not just 'doing'. It involves planning, organising and sequencing too, so cognition goes hand in hand with movement learning. Daily observations and movement practices can ensure that children don't get left out of games and ploys because they can't do the movements quickly or accurately enough. Moving effectively contributes to a high self-esteem.

Let's find out now what questions parents, carers and professionals ask about children's movement.

Q: What are the key movement competences?

A: Taken separately, the components are:

- *Strength*: this comes from having good muscle tone and many opportunities for practice.
- *Speed*: this involves making judgements about how fast to move in different environments. Too much speed can cause accidents and not enough speed can mean there is not enough momentum to get the job done.
- *Space*: this involves having spatial awareness and judging where to go and when. Learning about directions and distances is part of this component.
- *Balance*: balance comes from the vestibular sense and is a key component of every move that is made. It even works when the body is at rest. There are two kinds of balance – static (which helps control when the body is still) and dynamic (needed to aid control as the body moves).
- *Co-ordination*: this involves making different body parts work together to achieve a fluid action. The ability to cross the midline should always be checked since inability here compromises writing and many of the tasks of daily living such as cleaning teeth, tying shoe laces or ties.

When these underlying competences are efficient, they blend to produce movement that is rhythmical and free flowing. Where difficulties arise, there is 'too much' or 'too little' of one or the other. Too much strength would mean kicking the ball out of bounds or not being able to release small items from the pincer grip. Practitioners need to appreciate the separate components so that they can observe and assess which is causing difficulty and intervene with the correct kind of support, and remember to analyse the transitions that join the separate movements too.

It is important to remember that balanced and flowing movement depends on the correct selection of the above competences in relation to the movement task.

Q: What do you mean when you talk about movement for babies and toddlers? When I think about movement I think about running and jumping or even the PE programmes children do at school, but I hadn't thought about babies and movement. Why it is this so important?

A: Movement is much more than running, jumping and playing games, although these things are very important too, for they show that the children have learned to combine movements. In so doing they have not only acquired the separate movements (skills) but have coped with the transitions between them. Hopefully, then, the descriptors 'efficient' and 'effective' can be applied. Movement is part of everything we do from opening our eyes in the morning to getting dressed to playing with toys, and later speaking and writing. The movements babies do are building blocks that lead to the acquisition of more skilled movements later on. From a few days or weeks, babies can practise moving, e.g. reaching and stretching, kicking and waving, and later rolling over, learning to sit and, of course, learning to crawl then walk in a safe environment with someone close at hand to ensure they come to no harm. When babies achieve one skill, this acts as a spur to try the next one. Most children love to move and are intrinsically motivated to seek new challenges. Hazards abound but a sense of danger kicks in two weeks after the children learn to crawl, so that should relieve some of the pressure on anxious adults.

Movement even affects seeing clearly, for this depends on the muscles that control eye movements working together to give clear sight. At birth, babies have limited vision because there was no light in the womb, so receptors in the eyes were not stimulated. Lacking prenatal practice, therefore, babies may see best at feeding distance and for a little time have double vision. This clears as the baby's increasing strength allows the muscles controlling the eyes to work together to produce a single image. At 8–12 months or so, when babies begin mono-syllabic **babbling**, saying 'mama' or 'dada', this is a preliminary practice for articulating words clearly later on. It also provides strengthening for the muscles in the tongue and the lips, for clear speech requires co-ordination and control of 150 muscles.

Q: When people talk about strength, they usually think of the large muscle groups that support gross movements such as crawling or walking. But is strength important for fine movements such as building blocks, drawing and threading too?

A: Yes, indeed. These early practices stimulate the dexterity essential for later writing, and craft and art skills. The children have to learn how to control the amount of strength they need to grasp and release that strength in letting go.

Q: Is strength needed inside the body?

Figure 4.3 Children learning how to control their strength in grasping and then letting go

A: Yes. Muscle strength is also needed internally if the organs are to function well, e.g. the sphincter, a muscular ring at the entrance to the bladder has to contract and expand to control the escape of urine. This has to be working efficiently before babies can be potty trained. And, of course, the heart is a large muscle that needs strength to work rhythmically and continuously throughout life.

Q: What about muscle tone? Is that the same thing?

A: Generally, strength and muscle tone are seen as being synonymous. Muscle tone features in the birth assessment by the Apgar score. Babies who have good muscle tone are able to support their heads early; they have strong limbs and are responsive, i.e. they react to touch or sounds or lights. Floppiness or poor muscle tone that prevents this reaction may be a sign that the cerebellum is not functioning well, but again mothers need to give babies enough time to gain strength. After all, being born and thrust into a very strange world is a traumatic experience and time is needed to adjust to a new complex environment (Goddard Blythe 2008). Having said that, many mothers have told me that they knew from the beginning that there was something wrong because their baby was so floppy, so concerns about continuing poor muscle tone, perhaps into the second or third month, should be shared with a GP, health visitor, social worker, psychologist or physiotherapist.

Q: Obviously, most babies, toddlers and children become more and more skilled at moving as they grow. Is there a time line?

A: Strength develops from head to toe (**cephalocaudal**) and from centre to periphery (**proximodistal**). This explains why all babies hold their heads erect before they sit and sit before they stand. In the earliest months their legs are relatively weak and their trunks 'higher up' in the developmental sequence are stronger. This also explains why reaching and grasping needs practice. This is because fingers are at the periphery or edge of the stretch, so they are late to gain strength and control. This can be seen when babies have learned to grasp a rattle but have difficulty letting it go.

When parents, nurseries and other early years centres teach finger games such as 'Round and round the garden' or 'Incy Wincy spider', they are supporting peripheral movement development and aiding dexterity, especially when the babies copy the actions. These activities strengthen their fingers and help develop the pincer grip that will be necessary for picking up objects and holding them safely, as well as for writing later on. Less well known is the fact that each fingertip is connected to a large piece of tissue in the frontal cortex of the brain (Winkley 2004). This is the executive centre where problem-solving occurs. So, stimulating

Figure 4.4 Games such as 'Round and round the garden', apart from the bonding and enjoyment of repetition, also help children to be aware of their hands at the perimeter and to be sensitive to touch. They then learn how to handle objects with care

this area by encouraging finger activities promotes another direct link between moving and learning. Did you ever hear the expression that young children who played a musical instrument were good at maths? That might just be one reason why.

Q: What about before birth? Are movements important then?

A: At about four months gestation, the midwife will ask mothers-to-be if they have felt the baby moving. Answering 'yes' will reassure everyone that the baby is developing well. Babies also need time to sleep, however, so there will be periods of inactivity. As the baby grows there is less space in the womb to move around, so movement will be constrained. However, if there is prolonged quiet after kicking has been felt, it's best to check with the midwife or clinic nurse to make sure that all is well. (See also 'The importance of movement during the birth process' in Chapter 1.)

Q: I realise that babies begin learning even before they are born. I know they can hear and this is amazing, but movement? What sorts of things are they learning as they move?

A: When babies move in the womb, it is fascinating to find that they are learning about distance (how far can I stretch?) and directions (where can I go?); they are even learning about balance for the vestibular sense (the sense of balance) is working to enable them to get into the correct, head-down position ready for a vaginal birth. At this stage movement is within the confines of the womb, but these experiences will continue to develop after birth. All new babies can swim – they kick to propel themselves through the water, showing that they have practised this action before they were born. These prenatal practices also help them to know where they end and 'the outside world' begins. They are beginning to recognise their body boundary, a key component of the self-concept. So stepping-stones for developing a 'sense of self' also depend on movement learning. More and more psychologists are finding that this, i.e. developing a sense of self or, in psychological terms, 'a theory of mind', is a prerequisite for assessing others, so making decisions about choosing friends and building sound relationships. Early philosophers such as Socrates and Huxley were wise indeed when they penned the matrix, 'Know thyself'.

Q: And after the baby is born, what kinds of movements should we observe then? Are there charts to let us know the times when different movements should be possible? And are there things we can do to encourage our babies to move well?

A: There are three important issues here. Assessment charts give us pointers to monitor a baby's progress. Table 4.1 outlines the motor milestones.

Research claims that gifted and talented children are likely to achieve their milestones 30 per cent ahead of time, and that most gifted and talented children are always on the go. Very often parents find this overwhelming.

Table 4.1 Age-related patterns: the motor milestones

Age	Locomotor skills	Non-locomotor skills	Manipulative skills
Birth	Primitive walking reflex and swimming reflex, but these will disappear.	Will focus at feeding distance: hold eye contact.	May hold finger for a moment.
4 months	Can sit (briefly) if propped up. Enjoys baby massage and tummy time.	Plays with hands as first toy; will hold object briefly; head should be steady, hand-grip firm.	First attempts at passing objects from hand to hand. Plays with toes; puts toes in mouth.
6–9 months	Crawls speedily. Some children pull up to stand. Sense of danger evident (two weeks after crawling).	Sitting without support. Reaching and grasping more accurately now.	Holds toys; feeds self with bottle or finger food. Recognises that dropped objects are still there – seeks to retrieve them
9–12 months	Crawling, walking round furniture, crawling up stairs.	Shows preference for some toys; handles them carefully.	Scribbles holding pencil firmly. Everything goes into the mouth for testing texture and taste.
12–18 months	Walking securely. Will roll over and crawl as a combined action. Rhythmic 'dancing' to music.	Does simple puzzles; uses the pincer grip. Enjoys knocking toys over; cares for soft toys–first signs of shared empathy.	Will turn the pages of books. Independent feeding. Uses two hands independently.
18–24 months	Runs (20 months), walks well (24 months); climbs stairs with both feet on each step.	Pushes and pulls boxes or wheeled toys; unscrews lid on a jar.	Shows clear hand preference; stacks four to six blocks; turns pages one at a time; picks things up without overbalancing.
2–3 years	Runs easily. Climbs up, down and over obstacles unaided.	Enjoys drawing and painting with large brush.	Picks up small objects (e.g. fragments of paper or cereal). Throws small ball forward while standing.
3–4 years	Walks upstairs one foot per step; skips using alternate feet; walks on tiptoe.	Pedals and steers a tricycle. Walks in any direction pulling a big toy. Rotates body when throwing but still little body rotation.	Catches large ball between outstretched arms; cuts paper with scissors; holds pencil between thumb and first two fingers.

Age	Locomotor skills	Non-locomotor skills	Manipulative skills
4–5 years	Walks up and downstairs one foot per step; stands, runs and walks well. Combines actions seamlessly, e.g. run and jump.	Boys show mature throwing action; girls enjoy balance challenges such as ballet.	Strikes ball with bat; kicks and catches ball; threads beads but not needle; grasps pencil maturely.
5–6 years	Skips on alternate feet; walks a thin line; slides, swings.	More children show mature turning and kicking action.	Plays ball games quite well. Threads needle and sews stitches.

Q: What if my baby doesn't follow this sequence?

A: Before you worry, you have to remember that babies acquire different skills at different times. We have lively, seemingly fearless babies who won't be still and calm, cautious ones who are reluctant to take risks. We have 'big for their age babies' and those who have had to deal with illnesses or other hiccups that have caused developmental delay. We have children with disabilities and diseases, and those who have experienced abuse. We have children who have been brought up with the freedom to move, and others who have been constrained by shoes and buggies. This means that the 'normal' timing in achieving the movement patterns is quite wide. Mothers should never panic but seek reassurance and possibly physiotherapy if their baby's movement profile does not *roughly* match the norms.

The 'developmental norms' that feature in the charts are objective indicators of progress. They are derived from observations of thousands of children in many different cultures and environments. Always remember, however, that it is difficult to find one child who matches all the outcomes all of the time. What makes decision making about when to intervene hard is that development doesn't happen in a smooth curve. There are stops and starts and many surprises, probably down to the surge in myelin production (see p. 31), combined with the youngsters gaining confidence. This is what makes development so interesting and finding the right strategies to support individual children so challenging.

Q: If there are times when movements should be achieved, can we/should we urge our children on to achieve the next step?

A: This is an interesting question. The answer would be 'gently' if you are sure the baby is nearly there. Or, if you are unsure, the answer would have to be 'no', or at least be very cautious. In fact, attempting to rush might be ill-advised because babies have an inbuilt sequence of development that suits their stage of development. They will walk when they are ready, i.e. when they have the musculature and the co-ordination to do so. We really don't teach babies to walk. They are intrinsically motivated to do so. It may be that encouragement will give confidence to babies when they are nearly ready and the box 'can walk' can be ticked a little earlier, but learning cannot happen until children have the neurological development to allow this complex series of events to happen. Often parents just have to be patient. Babies can't achieve everything at once.

Q: Can you explain the intellectual side of moving a little more?

A: Learning to move is really problem solving. Children have to ask themselves questions such as 'What foot do I move first?' 'What do I do next?' 'How do I shift my balance and how fast should I go?' 'What will happen if I move quickly or run over there?' 'Will I be hurt if I fall?' The next time you go out in the snow, recognise the questions you are asking yourself as you go.

Q: What's the best way to encourage children to attempt new movements?

A: The ideal order of interventions to support the child would be:

- observe;
- encourage;
- plan how to intervene;
- lightly support the child;
- praise, and on the next attempt, reduce the support.

There are many interesting and valuable and simple things to do that will encourage babies to progress without stress.

Q: What are they?

A: Here are some ideas to try at birth to three months.

- Lie on the floor with baby on your front so that they can feel the rhythm of your breathing. Quietly sing a nursery rhyme and you will both feel relaxed. Early rhythmical opportunities are important for later reading and listening to stories and poems. After a while, move gently side to side, letting the baby feel the change of position and the move you make to regain balance.
- Let the baby lie on their back and kick with no nappy. They are learning about directions

and distances as they strengthen their legs. Whenever possible, let them be free from clothes so that they can fully exercise their arms and legs.

- Dangle a jingly toy so that they can practise stretching to catch it or kick it with their toes. When their limbs make contact with the toy, take a moment to praise, then perhaps clap, so that they recognise that they have been successful. Then they will be anxious to repeat the move and perhaps they will clap too. They are consolidating their understanding of 'body boundary', developing their early spatial awareness and working at the midline of their body.

- At this age your baby's movements are not well co-ordinated. Watch how their arms flail around, but often their hands are strong. Allow your baby to grip your finger, looking at them and singing as you do. This is a game you can play together. Try this with both his hands and feel if one grips more strongly than the other. The baby will have difficulty letting go, which is usual. Movement and communication should always go together.

It is important not to pull a baby up by the fingertip hold. Unless their back and neck muscles are really strong, their head will flop back, causing distress and possibly damage.

You can try the following. With your arm bent at 90 degrees, clench your fist hard. Feel how the strength and tension goes right up your arm to your shoulder. As your baby grasps your finger, they will feel this too, and become stronger. Now stretch your arm out and clench your fist again. Can you feel how different this is? This explains how movement on the periphery is less efficient and why a baby has difficulty controlling movements there. It is best to check that baby's arms are at a 90-degree angle and not outstretched.

Make sure you give baby some tummy time every day, increasing the length of time to suit the baby's ability to support their head. Babies now sleep on their backs and so miss time on their tummies. However, it is important for babies to try to push up as this action will strengthen their arms and shoulders as well as their neck muscles. At first, babies will only hold this position for a moment or two because of their heavy heads, but gradually the time will increase and they can look out to view their world from a different perspective. After all, staring at the ceiling doesn't provide them with much stimulation.

Overhead mobiles that are too close to the cot or bed, or too brightly coloured can cause stress, so careful planning is needed if your baby is to enjoy them and be stimulated to reach out.

If your baby sucks their thumb, note in your baby book which hand they choose and later, see if this corresponds to their being right- or left-handed. Some babies even suck their thumb in the womb. At three to four months, your baby will be playing with their hands. This is a very important stage. Help them to feel where their hands are by gently rubbing them together and then help them do a clapping action. This helps develop body awareness. Make a rhythmical jingle – clap and clap, and clap and rub – repeat or sing several times and if the baby is enjoying the game, make the action larger so that they stretch to the side. Let them see you are enjoying the game. If your baby claps by themselves, copy what they do – this is a great way to hold their interest.

When babies lie on their backs, and especially if they are not hampered by a nappy, they will try, or should be encouraged to roll over, because this places them in a natural crawling position. If they are reluctant, gently cross one leg over to begin the action for them at eight months or so. They will soon get the idea. They also love the feeling of independence this brings – 'I can do things for myself, at last!' This practice is a precursor to crawling, a critically important developmental milestone.

Begin to play Peek-a-boo, although babies may not join in until they are 12 months or so. Hold a cloth just in front of their eyes, then pull it away until they understand the game. Then put it over your face, lean forward and encourage the baby to pull the cloth from your head. Say 'boo' gently at first. This develops turn taking (the basis of language) and also reaching and grasping. Babies may still have difficulty letting go, but this is absolutely fine.

At five to seven months some babies will be sitting with support. Whether they can sit independently or not, it is a good idea to support them with cushions because heavy heads may cause them to topple backwards. But sitting is important because then they have a different view of the world from lying down and because their arms are free to reach and grasp. This allows them to hold toys and begin to feed with finger food. Check whether baby's grasping action is more direct now. When they reach for a toy or a spoon, is their action more purposeful and efficient? Encourage them to reach out in different directions and check whether they can stretch over the midline of their bodies.

To give practice in tracking, i.e. eye movements that follow a moving object, hold a toy just out of reach so that the baby has to stretch out – sideways, crossing over, above their head, and so on. This helps them to feel the balance needed to sit without support. Again, this is best without a nappy. Some babies will follow the toy with their eyes rather than reaching out. That is fine – this is a tracking check rather than a reaching and grasping one.

Hold the baby's attention by dropping a feather from just above head height. Blow it in the air so that the baby has time to watch, then reach and grasp. Once the baby has understood what is happening, drop the feather slightly behind so that they have to turn their head and shoulders. This immediately adds a balance challenge. Through activities like this, babies learn to lose and regain their balance. This gives them confidence in being able to regain a balanced position and helps them to estimate risk taking later on.

At eight to nine months a toy or a tower of bricks placed just out of reach will encourage a sitting baby to move from the spot. Getting started can be difficult if legs, stretched in front, get tangled up. This is a good example of how movement planning must precede action. This is even more perplexing if a baby is tied up in a nappy, so a spell of bare-bottom play helps them to get the feel of how to change position from sitting to crawling. This is hard work because legs have to be manoeuvred out of the way and, even when the crawling position is achieved, the weight of a baby's head means that first attempts often result in moving backwards. This is frustrating for the child but is a natural stepping-stone to achieving a more effective crawling action.

Tummy time for babies who are nearly crawling is very important. Some mothers report that at first their babies are rather reluctant to be placed on their fronts, but they soon recognise that they can see more and do more in that position, and then they begin to roll over for themselves. Watch them carefully and see them get stronger.

- Rolling over from back to front gets babies into a natural crawling position and this allows them to have a different, more interesting and active view of their world. Roll a soft ball towards the baby and they will soon reach out to pick it up. This is good practice for timing a moving object and tracking its path.
- Lying on their front encourages the baby to push up and so strengthens their arm, back and neck muscles, leading to better control of the head. At first holding the head erect

is tiring and will only be sustained for brief spells. However, if the baby starts to tire, they will simply collapse flat on the floor or roll onto their back again or let you know they are uncomfortable. No harm will have been done.

In sitting, allow your baby to investigate a treasure basket and discover for themselves what things can do (Hughes 2010).

- The treasure basket can hold things like measuring spoons that give a pleasing jingle when shaken and this encourages further exploration. A whole variety of household objects such as washed-out plastic bottles (clear ones can have a little coloured liquid added to encourage tipping and tilting so the baby notices the effect on the liquid), wooden spoons of different lengths, tins to bang and small containers of different shapes and sizes. As the baby mouths the different objects – and they will, because this is how they discover the properties of objects, i.e. whether they are hard or soft or rigid or flexible and whether they taste good, they are reaching and grasping, and in mouthing, bringing the object to the midline of the body. They are also problem-solving, e.g. 'What can this do?', 'Does it make a noise?', 'Is it hard or soft?', 'Does it change shape?'

Q: What should I observe?

A: Carefully observe the movements the baby makes as they lift and replace objects, hold them up high or try to roll them. They are developing the three magic competences – i.e. balance, co-ordination and control – and learning about spatial concepts such as distance, space and direction. These develop through answering questions such as, 'How far can I reach out before I topple over?', 'When does the wooden block get too heavy to hold?', 'Does it pull me over?', How do I adjust to stop this happening?' and eventually, 'How do I let it go?'. Letting go is hard, but gradually dropping is replaced by placing. This is a real sign of motor progress. Watch for the change.

Babies gradually recognise that objects behave in different ways and even more importantly that they themselves are in charge of making something happen. This leads to repetitive behaviour that gives babies time to study cause and effect. This is real learning, so give them plenty of time to explore.

Be amazed at the unusual ways babies find in handling objects – they are not limited by perceptions of how things should be done. This is the very earliest creative endeavour. Let them explore, find things out for themselves and see how they concentrate.

Q: Where should I sit when all this is happening?

A: Don't! Get down on the floor and hold eye contact. Positioning yourself in relation to what the baby is trying to achieve is important. Crouch down beside the baby to give them

Figure 4.5 Rachael shows how tummy time helps to strengthen her whole body

confidence to try new things and, if they seem willing to try, offer a little support to encourage progress. Hum or sing jingles to hold their attention and encourage them to listen.

While we all want our babies to be safe, we must not smother their efforts to move. There will be bumps as they try to walk, but bottoms are usually protected by nappies. This is one good time to wear one.

Crawling using the cross-lateral pattern (one hand and the opposite knee forward) is a key developmental milestone. It helps co-ordination, balance and spatial orientation, and the pattern shows that unnecessary primitive reflexes have not been retained.

It is a good idea to think of different activities that provide opportunities to develop cross-lateral work. Climbing up stairs or climbing frames lets observers see whether the cross-lateral pattern has been achieved.

Children must have the necessary strength and co-ordination before they can walk. It is an inbuilt maturational process. Children won't walk until they are ready.

In walking there should be a smooth heel–toe action, showing a transfer of weight that propels the body forward. As babies learn to walk they have a wide-apart, feet side-by-side action, but this should change to a forward propulsive action as balance is achieved. It is important to observe this because 'a strange gait' can be an early sign of additional needs and early intervention is called for. A persisting stilted gait *may* show a neurological weakness.

Table 4.2 Activities to develop opportunities for cross-lateral work

Activity	Look for	Support
First, ask the children to take up the crawling (table) position. This is a safe position where balance is not difficult. The children feel secure.	Children who can't keep a flat back. Wobbly limbs – arms or legs. Children who sit back or topple to the side when they look up.	Place a beanbag on the small of the back – ask the children to keep it steady there. Crawl alongside the baby to show how it's done. Emphasise strong arms and legs.
Move the body from side to side or forwards and backwards if they can, keeping the beanbag in position. Then they can try to toss the beanbag off by straightening their legs. They should always come back to the crawling (table) position.	Children who can't regain the table position after moving – they may have to sit back or their arms may collapse.	Strengthening work for arms and legs. Check if children can't move their weight forward onto arms that should stay straight and strong.
In the table position again, the children can pick up beanbags from the floor and toss them into a bin.	This means one arm moves and the weight adjusts to balance on three limbs. This helps them to learn: a) to keep balanced when one limb moves and b) gives them some idea about direction and distance.	They can score a point when the beanbag goes in. For progressions, ask the children to move further back from the bin. Circles drawn round the bin can give scoring targets.
Stand close in to the side of your child who is in the crawling position and ask them to push you over.	Pushing against your legs will give resistance and strengthen the muscles in the trunk. Make sure you do this at both sides of the body to strengthen equally.	
Encourage crawling every day – up stairs, over obstacles, under tables.	Climbing over obstacles or up stairs uses the same pattern. It is often easier to observe the cross-lateral pattern then.	

Q: What should we do?

A: Allow the children to go barefoot on safe surfaces whenever possible.

If shoes must be worn, check the soles to see they are flexible, allowing the correct action – i.e. a transfer from heel to toe. Many shoes prevent this.

- As often as possible encourage children to walk barefoot without shoes, on different surfaces, e.g. along pavements, at the edge of the sea, on rough paths and smooth grasses.
- Play a game using fairy steps and giant steps, gentle steps and bouncy steps, because such practices all need different types of balance and control.

- Older children (three years) enjoy follow-my-leader games when the leader chooses to march or jog or run on the spot. The leader decides on/calls out/ demonstrates tasks – e.g. hold your hands on your head as you go etc. Change the leader regularly and repeat with jogging or skipping once the routine is known.
- Make a circuit with whatever equipment suits the children's competence. Add obstacles, e.g. skittles to walk or run round, benches or other balance equipment such as stepping stones, ropes making a wiggly worm on the ground, tunnels to crawl through, changing the layout as competence grows.
- Practise stalking and tracking as a quiet-as-a-mouse activity. This encourages children to be aware of the way they are placing their feet on the floor and the heel to toe transfer is emphasised in the slower action.

Q: When should my baby have shoes?

A: Shoes are really unnecessary until the baby is walking well and needs protection from rough surfaces. Shoes constrict the feet and also prevent the baby experiencing the different textures that are underfoot. In cold weather warm socks are better than shoes if they have special non-slip soles.

Q: How can I record my child's progress?

A: A good idea is to make a timetable of when you saw your baby (comfortably and securely at home) achieve the movements that are outlined on the movement chart. If you suspect that physiotherapy may be required, a good idea is to video the baby trying to carry out different movements (gross and fine skills). This provides an objective record and each entry is dated, then parents and professionals have a record of change over time. Photos are good too, but they don't provide a moving image. Even an image on a phone can be helpful in showing where difficulties occur. These can facilitate communications with a physiotherapist and save emotional parents stress.

Q: To finish, can you summarise the competences again?

A: Balance from the vestibular sense is working when we are moving and when we are still. The movement receptors, or proprioceptors, all over our bodies are taking information from the environment and relaying it through the central nervous system to the brain for analysis and action. Balance is part of everything we do. The boy in the picture opposite could not have trundled the heavy tyre without a good sense of balance, giving him stability and control.

Figure 4.6 Lee is showing how strength and balance together enable him to wheel the tyre

Balance is important even when writing. The feet should be supported on the floor or on a block because swinging legs can cause tilting and the whole body loses control. So, if writing difficulties become apparent, check the child's balance first.

There are different types of co-ordination. Hand–eye co-ordination is needed in activities such as aiming or catching a ball or threading beads. Foot–eye co-ordination is needed in many sports, e.g. in skiing and football. Whole-body co-ordination is required in dancing, gymnastics and swimming. If co-ordination is difficult, then simplifying the task can help, e.g. allowing the child to sit to draw and paint takes away the balance challenges and allows concentration on the task at hand. Providing swimming aids is another support and allowing practices of kicking goals without the worry of a goalie works, too. In this way the child internalises the pattern of the skill without added stressors.

Control happens when the child selects the correct amount of speed, strength and space. This supports their ability to balance. Strangely, children who find movements difficult often try to go faster and then all control is lost. Slowing the movement and giving explanations of the demands of each part helps the planning as well as the doing. Also, reducing distractors in the environment, such as practising catching a ball in a quiet space with the child looking at a plain background, helps.

Being able to move well is hugely important to children. They want to tie their laces and ride their bikes at the same time as their friends. Ensuring that the basics of movement are attained at the right, critically important time helps ensure that children will be able to do all the things they want to do. Practice ensures that they will grow in confidence as well as in competence in movement, and this will transfer to all aspects of their learning.

Chapter 5

The earliest learning

'Learning' is a broad term that covers almost everything we do. We learn about our family; we learn to make a friend; we learn to move and to speak, to sing, and to laugh and to cry. We learn to remember and to forget, to love and to hate, to rejoice and to despair. Learning begins even before we are born and carries on until we die. How we do this is guided by the competences and temperamental traits we have inherited, by the motivation we have to learn more things and by the sharing of the family beliefs, structures and environmental experiences in which we grow. This is known as social transmission. Learning is an active process – a kind of interactive partnership between children, the family, and its wider social network that includes nurseries, family and children's centres, and eventually schools. This environment is the setting in which children learn to interact and build on their initial understandings and experiences in increasingly complex ways. Development happens when the body and brain work together to make new thinking and learning, and therefore new achievements, possible. Some children will learn at an amazing speed, others will take longer and they will all have their own preferred ways. When adults choose to intervene to teach them something, they have to gauge the child's readiness to absorb the 'instructions' necessary to allow them to carry out a new task. This is what makes observation and assessment, i.e. finding what makes each child tick, so complex but so fascinating.

Q: There are so many skills and competences that children must tackle. How can we keep track of them all?

A: That is why, for purposes of study and research, it is a good idea to subdivide development into four aspects, i.e. social, emotional, intellectual and motor. In each, researchers have studied very many children across cultures, and their findings have been collated to give 'developmental norms' which provide evidence of what children should be able to do at different stages. These, along with particular knowledge of each child's likes, dislikes and general competencies, build a picture of 'readiness' so that individual children can enjoy success in their new learning challenges.

Let's divide playing in the house corner by these headings.

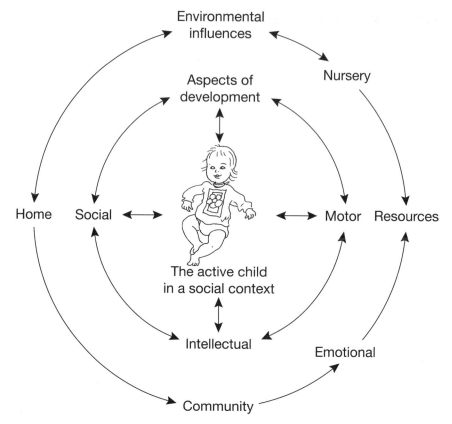

Figure 5.1 The interacting aspects of development

Social development — Working co-operatively; preparing meals; setting places at table, preparing meals for others at the table carefully; being pleasant and helpful; offering food, giving others choices; turn taking and sharing.

Motor development – Preparing and cutting food; balancing plates; talking on the telephone; dressing the doll; enjoying the meal; dialling the telephone; tidying; being responsible; tying aprons; making a meal.

Emotional development — Acting out roles; recognising; tidying up; balancing dishes; taking lead roles; playing subservient roles; gaining confidence in interacting; preparing a matching table (aesthetic appreciation); coping with disagreements and reaching a compromise.

Intellectual development — Caring for baby; learning to pretend and role play; one-to-one correspondence (is there a plate for every doll?); choice of dishes; tablecloth, colour, shape; appreciation of planning and making a meal – presentation and 'looking good'; choosing ingredients for healthy eating; selecting suitable clothes for a doll either in terms of weather or fashion language, e.g. responding to suggestions, giving alternative ideas; making a meal, following a simple recipe.

People who study development recognise that such a division might be considered artificial because progress or regression in one aspect affects them all, but it is one way of making the study manageable.

Let's consider an emotional characteristic on the competence list, e.g. being confident. Confident children are more likely to approach tasks with no hesitation and that means they find a place in the front row to watch or follow instructions. So they have a better chance of grasping the intricacies of the skill or, if they don't, they will be able to ask for further support. So their emotional competence spills over into the intellectual and motor aspects. Socially, too, confident, outgoing children are more likely to be sought out by friends and this helps their skills of interaction. They learn to share and take turns, and to give and receive praise for their efforts. They also practise interpreting the non-verbal communication of others.

Q: Is this something children have to learn?

A: Gradually, with experience, most children learn to interpret the body language and facial expressions of others, and these influence their decision-making. They learn about approval from seeing smiles and nods, and desist when frowns and shaking heads appear. It is fascinating to recognise that 90 per cent of the meaning in a message is conveyed non-verbally, which explains why children who cannot read the non-verbal communication of others are left isolated and unsure. This is the fate of children who have **autism**, a debilitating condition whereby children and adults withdraw from social encounters because nothing they see makes sense. They can be socially and emotionally isolated for all of their lives.

As you can see, understanding learning is a complex affair, dependent on the opportunities and support the children have, as well as the intrinsic and learned competences they bring to the challenge. Luckily, babies are primed to learn (Dowling 2004); they have an inbuilt motivation to absorb, retain and use perceptual information, i.e. what they see, hear, touch, taste and smell, and in so doing they re-combine new meanings for themselves. Parents, practitioners and teachers are there to support and encourage this miraculous endeavour.

Let's ask parents first what they want to know about their child's learning or intellectual development.

Q: It's becoming apparent that the environment in which children grow will be important in nurturing their learning. Has there been research on the psychological side of things rather than providing resources? I ask that because I see very some some very unhappy children coming out of centres. They can be angry and upset or crying fiercely. Obviously, the adults can't cope and the children are learning that this is an unhappy place. Have you any advice?

A: Sutherland (2006) has researched what she calls 'The key relational needs of the child.' She advises on the best strategies if there is any conflict or tension. She analyses the child's needs into four categories, which she calls

- attunement;
- validation of how the child is experiencing the event;
- containment of feelings;
- soothing or tension regulation.

These needs would seem to be particularly relevant for children who have or are meeting new challenges and perhaps are unsure of their status.

Q: What do the terms mean?

A: Let's describe them in turn.

Attunement

The secret of gaining attunement is to understand the child's emotional intensity and to meet that by engaging with them at an appropriate level. So, if the child shows despair, then the adult has to articulate their understanding of the child's feelings, spelling out their commitment in trying to understand and to offer support. This may mean waiting until an outburst has passed, but the child should be aware that the adult is waiting sympathetically, ready to respond and do what is best to find a solution.

It can be very difficult for adults to know how to react, especially if the child won't share their feelings and rebuffs attempts to pacify them. Useful advice about not overwhelming the child by proffering too many alternatives or solutions too soon needs to be considered too. A period of shared silence can often lead to calm, allowing more rational discussion.

Validation of how the child is experiencing the event

This means trying to see events from the child's perspective and empathising with what they are experiencing. In this way the adult is confirming what the child has endured. This is different from trying to distract the child or jolly them out of their unhappiness, or to make light of the trauma in an effort to dispel grief. Adults need to find the words to convey that they appreciate what the child is going through and that they recognise that physical symptoms such as a sore tummy is just as painful when the cause is psychological or emotional rather than down to illness. So comments such as 'I know that was a terrible thing to have happened and I do understand why you are so upset. Remember, you are safe now,' may give comfort. Even though they may not produce an immediate positive response, the child may retain the nuance and reflect at a calmer time later on.

Containment of feelings

This results from adults staying with the situation and not being diverted by outside events, which is then interpreted by the child as being more important or more worthy of their attention. The adults must also stay in control of feelings of anger, which the child's distress may engender. If, for example, being bullied at nursery distresses the already vulnerable child – and yes, children can be bullied in the nursery – the adult has to stay calm and focused while trying to prepare a plan of action that is acceptable to the child. Overly expressed anger or dismay does not foster containment; nor do comments such as 'Well, bullies are there all the time – it's a fact of life. Listening and/or waiting calmly is a good first step.

Allied to this is the setting of boundaries. If children overstep the mark, then explanations and joint discussions should precede any 'punishment' such as limiting time at a favourite activity. In a new setting children will meet new rules and boundaries, or their first setting at home may have been so erratic that it gave no sense of security and then 'right' and 'wrong' becomes confused. Sutherland describes children without boundaries as being 'limit deprived'.

Soothing or tension regulation

To try to support children through their intense feelings of stress/ worthlessness/anomie, adults need to use a calm constant approach, using touch to comfort if this is acceptable. Of course, children who are very sensitive and those who have been abused may see touch or a hug as a precursor to further hurt. At nursery, adults should ask the child if a cuddle would help. Stay calm if it is rejected or if the suggestion brings on screams. (Adults, please check on the region's policy on touching children.) Another recommendation is to hold eye contact, but again this can be difficult for children who find it difficult to read responses or who find proximity threatening. The aim is that children will learn to self-regulate their emotions rather than becoming aggressive or harming themselves, both of which are signs of despair.

Q: If children constantly have outbursts and seem inconsolable, what then? What is going on and are there likely to be long-lasting effects?

A: These children must be under tremendous stress and Winston (2004: 448) explains, 'Stress is perhaps the most classic and common example of the way a state of mind can affect the body.' He also points out that the ability to handle stress is vital because, left unchecked or continuing for a time, it can be linked to many illnesses. This is because substances such as cortisol can affect the body's ability to fight infection. Cortisol is helpful in the short term as it helps the body to react to a stimulus; it helps energy to be mobilised, but long term, it causes tiredness and even depression. This is because it blocks GABA (the emotional chemical that calms the nervous system) and so prevents the stressed person from being able to self-calm. Aggression can result. When cortisol floods the frontal cortex of the brain it can prevent reasoning and problem-solving taking place, and anguish can be expressed as anger.

Children raised with a 'gentle touch' approach will produce increased amounts of serotonin – the happy hormone – resulting in lower levels of aggression. This will enable them to be positive and more resilient in meeting new people and confronting new experiences. When they have lower levels of stress, they are likely to be healthier. So sustaining a gentle approach with calmly stated boundaries has particular benefits for children confronting new experiences and challenges.

Q: Some children cope with huge problems and keep smiling, while others are naturally withdrawn or unwilling to try anything new, even though they may both come from very supportive homes. Why should this be?

A: Children inherit fundamentally different ways of coping. These are known as temperamental traits and they affect the way children perceive their world and as a result how they behave. These traits or spontaneous ways of behaving can be seen on a continuum and while they can be modified by environmental factors such as explanations of ways to cope, in new and/or challenging situations children tend to revert to their intrinsic mode. Very often environmental factors are not strong enough to overcome the innate traits. There are three key traits, usually expressed as polar constructs, but in effect functioning as a continuum.

Table 5.1 Some temperamental traits

Extrovert: sunny, outgoing.	Introvert: shy, private, withdrawn
Resilient: bounces back; sees the best in events – the glass is half full.	Vulnerable: easily hurt, tends to see the downside; the glass is half empty.
Impulsive: acts without considering the consequences.	Reflective: ponders on many possibilities or outcomes before acting.

Many more traits could expand this list, which is why Thomas and Chess (1977) claimed that just three descriptors covered all eventualities. They are 'The extrovert, the introvert and the slow-to-warm up child.'

Q: Would this be why my two-year-old non-identical twins are as different as chalk and cheese, and why they argue and scrap so much?

A: Well, of course, two-year-olds are renowned for wanting more independence than they can cope with and screaming their frustration when it is denied, and you have this twofold. But certainly, temperamental traits make a big contribution to how children think and act, and as they are inherited, then each child receives a different set from the gene pool. These can be modified as children mature and gain confidence from successfully meeting new challenges. Generally speaking, very young children are impulsive. They act without considering the consequences. This is why mothers and early years staff claim they need eyes in the back of their heads. However, most children become more reflective as they mature and even learn to mentally rehearse the way they will respond. Perhaps this involves anticipating the consequences, a skill based on previous experiences or perhaps discussions with parents or carers about the best way to behave.

In most children, the frontal cortex of the brain that helps control logical reasoning is not fully functional until adolescence, so these children will retain their impulsiveness longer. In extreme cases of impulsiveness, this trait makes a significant contribution to the condition ADD (attention deficit disorder) and can be a part of dyspraxia, dyslexia and autism.

Resilient children can overcome disadvantages that would overwhelm their more vulnerable peers. They see the best; they focus on the positive; they bounce back when their more vulnerable friends are left distressed. This is why two children can genuinely have very different accounts of events. So 'He bullied me' can be countered by 'I was just playing', and both children believe they are telling the truth. Some resilient children from homes where abuse is the norm can survive horrors that would leave more vulnerable children distraught. On the other hand, vulnerable children from advantaged homes can be unhappy and feel aggrieved despite all their resources and support.

Q: This discussion has raised the question of discerning the comparative parts that nature (or the genetic blueprint we inherit from our parents) and nurture (or the environmental effects such as relationships and resources) play in development. How is this considered in relation to IQ?

A: The nature/nurture debate is hotly contested in relation to intelligence. Questions such as, 'Is there a gene for genius?' and 'Is intelligence born or made? are constantly under review and regularly provide conflicting answers. In his study of identical twins who share the same gene pool, Thomson (2001) discovered that each had exactly the same ratio of **grey matter** to **white matter** in their brains and this corresponded to them having identical IQ scores. Non-identical twins with varying amounts of white and grey matter scored differently in IQ tests. This suggested that our genes play a significant part in determining the amount of grey matter (neurons or thinking cells) we have and therefore in determining how intelligent we are. So is intelligence a fixed entity or can it be changed? Are we stuck with what we've been given? Professor Donald McIntyre of Oxford University often urged his students to further effort by claiming 'anyone can do anything provided they want it hard enough'. This suggested that, with enough commitment, all ambitions could be fulfilled. Winston (2004) is equally convinced that 'whatever your genetic inheritance, your way of life and environment can play a big part in determining your intelligence and how long it lasts'. He attests that keeping mentally and physically active can enhance the neuronal connections in the brain that give intelligence. Both recognise that intelligence is not a fixed entity but emphasise the ongoing commitment that is needed if children are to be highly successful. Gagne's (2001) model of giftedness and talent portrays talent as coming from committed practice. Certainly, he claims that this is aided by 'being very able in the first place' but he recognises that some gifted people, despite having support and resources, may not exercise their abilities and so not develop the talented performance that could have been theirs. This shows the effect of nature over nurture. Thankfully, studies of babies with a learning difference such as Down's syndrome show that with stimulation and regular, appropriate input, they can do much better than their condition (a fairly low IQ) would suggest. This shows the impact of nurture over nature.

Studies of babies of depressed mothers who have not given adequate stimulation to their children show that their babies have less activity in the left frontal cortex of their brains and practitioners have to try to compensate for a poor start. The earlier this intervention comes the more impact it will have, more so if the children are motivated to learn. So professionals can take heart in recognising that, no matter how poor the inheritance, with time and patience and a range of strategies, they can enhance the learning of each and every child.

Q: When we look at our six-month-old baby, we see him gurgling and watching us as we move. But he has such a lot to learn. How can he do this?

A: Jean Piaget (1952), the father of modern psychology, set out to research this question and although other researchers would accuse him of not considering the social effects on learning, Piaget's findings have stood the test of time, sourced many subsequent pieces of research, and guided educationalists about the appropriateness and timing of giving new learning. He claimed that children constructed their own understanding of the world and they did that through building ever more elaborate schemas. He argued that babies begin their lives with a small number of sensory and motor schemas such as looking, tasting, touching, reaching, listening and grasping. So, using their looking and grasping schema in contemplating objects, they recognise the shape of an orange as being similar to a ball and they add these observations to their understanding of round ball-like shapes. This involves the baby adding the new to the known, a process called **assimilation**. Once this is done, the schema becomes the foundation for comparisons, e.g. an orange looks like but does not taste like a ball. So the initial schema doesn't fit and the baby must adapt. This discovery affects how the child will act towards each object. Will they bite the ball? They will because mouthing is the way that babies learn about the properties of objects but perhaps they will do this only once. When the child discovers that the properties of the ball and the orange mean that they move in different ways, the next development is **accommodation**. This means that the baby is changing a schema as a result of assimilation and this is real learning. A third Piagetan term is **equilibration** and again this is a process, bringing accommodation and assimilation into balance. It is very important for parents and professionals to recognise this. Equilibration is when children restructure their schema to create a balance between assimilation and accommodation.

Put very simply, children begin with a few schemas. Gradually, experience causes them to extend and change their existing range. When differences are recognised, children modify their existing schemas by comparing the new to the old and adapting, even rejecting an original schema. However, children can't go on learning new things until they have had time and opportunity to make the comparison and adapt. If they are expected to do this too quickly, then stress may result; if there is not enough stimulation, then boredom results. Piaget believed that the process of equilibration is balance; in his words, 'it is an inborn automatic response to conflicts between children's current schemes and the challenges of the environment' (Bee and Boyd 2005: 149).

Piaget identified three equilibration points in childhood; the first two are appropriate for this text. These stages correspond to the time when experience, growth and maturation enable the child to do more things. These he named as the sensori-motor stage (birth to 18 months), when infants use their sensory and motor schema to make sense of and act upon their world.

At this stage new babies are tied to the here and now. They respond to stimuli that they are offered, e.g. smiling and stretching to reach a favourite toy, but they do not appear to remember much or plan ahead, although this is very difficult to prove. They mouth objects to find their texture and malleability as well as their taste. Some babies will relish biting into citrus fruits and others will screw up their faces and protest. Gradually, as memories develop, however, their repertoire of appropriate behaviours extends.

Children never seem to tire of repetition and, at 18 months, some will protest at any attempt by adults to miss out bits from stories. This shows how good their memories are, yet most adults find it hard to recapture events from when they were younger than three years old. As children grow and their nervous system matures, they are enabled to do more things. They recognise and remember more people and favourite foods, too, and increasingly make their likes and dislikes felt.

Q: Could you talk a bit more about how the senses help children to learn?

A: Sally Goddard describes the learning process well. She explains that

> All learning takes place in the brain, but it is the body which acts as the vehicle by which knowledge is acquired. Both brain and body work together through the central nervous system and both are dependent on the senses for all information about the outside world.
> (Goddard 1996: 41)

In so writing, she is explaining that learning involves three basic systems. These are:

the reception of incoming stimuli by the senses (the **afferent** system);
the processing or analysing of that information in the brain;
the lightning response to that analysis shown by actions (the **efferent** system).

To learn effectively, all three parts of the learning cycle must function effectively and, when learning proves difficult, practitioners – or, if the difficulty is severe, specific professionals such as physiotherapists or speech therapists – must discover which part of the cycle is breaking down. Some children can be hypersensitive or hyposensitive, i.e. over- or under-sensitive to each sensory input, and each of these extremes can cause learning difficulties. It may seem strange to claim that a child hearing too much or seeing too much is as disabled as a child who cannot hear or see enough, but some hypersensitive children cannot cut out distractors in the environment, so their day is composed of too much sound or display and both of these can cause children to withdraw from learning altogether.

Q: Aren't there five senses – hearing, seeing, tasting, touching and smelling?

A: All of these are certainly important, but there are others that are equally, even more fundamental to learning.

The sensory system is part of the nervous system. The sensory receptors take information from the external environment through seeing, hearing and feeling – i.e. through the visual, auditory and tactile senses and those of taste and smell – and through the less well-known internal ones – i.e. the vestibular, kinaesthetic and proprioceptive senses.

The vestibular sense, or sense of balance, is at 'the core of functioning' (Goddard 1996: 42), because all other senses pass through the vestibular mechanism at brain stem level. Therefore, input from all the other senses must be matched to the vestibular before their information can be processed accurately. The vestibular is the first sense to function and even in the womb it is important in getting the baby in the head-down position ready to be born. From then on it works to allow any change in posture or alignment. The vestibular system could be compared to having an internal compass that tells us about directions, e.g. forward, up, down, sideways, and allows the body to adapt in a controlled manner.

The vestibular sense also helps to ascertain hand and foot dominance which is important in writing and in all forms of habitual movement patterning. There are two kinds of balance – dynamic balance that keep us steady as we reach out or walk on uneven paths, and static

Table 5.2 The senses

The senses	Their key role	Indicators of difficulties
Vestibular	Balance	Unsteadiness; unwilling to leave the ground or take risks.
Kinaesthetic	Spatial awareness	Unable to judge distances; bumping and spilling.
Proprioceptive	Body awareness	General clumsiness
Visual	Seeing and tracking (functional sight)	Squinting; rubbing eyes; holding a book too near or far from the face.
Auditory	Listening and hearing	Distractibility; inability to focus.
Tactile	Feeling and touching	Needs firm touch or can't bear to be touched. Difficulties with judging personal space.
Taste and smell	Accepts/rejects food	Unwilling to try foods: Upset by smells. Restricted diet.

balance that keeps us secure when we are still. In activities such as ballet or sports, particularly extreme sports, the participants get great satisfaction from challenging their sense of balance, but if they are to be safe, they won't overcome it.

The following difficulties and observation points indicate a poor vestibular sense:

- A poor sense of balance: walk backwards in front of the child holding two hands and gradually release the hold as confidence grows.
- Motion sickness: as above, but walk over uneven paths or very gently push the child on a swing.
- Dislike of quick changes of direction: give timely warnings and allow mental preparation of what is to happen; practise walking on a curved path through skittles, then substitute a path with sharp turns.
- Avoidance of funfairs or playgrounds: revisit the swing park and encourage tolerance of swings and roundabouts.
- Being easily disoriented: keep the environment calm and unflustered.
- Bumping and dropping things: sometimes, but not all the time, ask the child to redo the task and explain. Ask the child to take more time as rushing can cause accidents too.
- Difficulty in staying still: only ask for very short periods of stillness. At story time, give the child something to stroke or squeeze. This will help to focus attention.

Figure 5.2 Gilly uses a wide stance and stretches her arms and hands out to help her balance

Babies hold their arms out to walk and have their legs wide apart to provide a more stable base, then with practice and maturity they gradually come to adopt the heel–toe action that gives fluency and economy and speed. Any delay in gaining balance should be investigated because it is so important in all kinds of actions.

The kinaesthetic and proprioceptive are two of the vital but less well known senses. However, to be accurate, the kinaesthetic sense only comes into play when there is muscle contraction, i.e. when the body is moving. The proprioceptive sense works all the time, relaying positional information when the body is moving or at rest. Proprioceptors are all over the body and in the muscles and joints. They are even located in the hair follicles and literally tell us where we end and the outside world begins. Children with a poor pro-prioceptive sense often have difficulty being still. They have to move so that their kinaesthetic and proprioceptive senses provide them with more secure information about where they are in space and contribute to making them feel balanced.

The following difficulties and observation points indicate a poor kinaesthetic or pro-prioceptive sense:

- A poor sense of poise, e.g. the child who has to slump over the table or high-chair tray and later at school, over the desk: work on strengthening the trunk, e.g. encourage the child to hold a strong table position in crawling.
- Easily tired by the constant effort needed to stay erect: give regular periods of time to relax: give regular periods of chill-out time.
- Constant movement and fidgeting: provide a beanbag to sit on and something to squeeze.
- Poor depth perception causing stumbling or 'falling over thin air': check the child's shoes and allow lots of movement in bare feet because this allows access to the proprioceptors there.
- Poor sense of direction: rehearse 'where to go' ahead of the child having to do so independently.
- Poor body awareness: play 'Simon says' types of games (for ideas, see *Jingle Time* (Macintyre 2003)).

A good plan is to involve the child in estimating distances. Place two ropes parallel on the floor with the child standing beside and ask, 'How many big/small/ giant steps do you think you'll need to get to the other side?' Then try in a fun way.

The visual sense

Assessing vision should cover much more than distance vision that is often the main concern in a simple eye test. Children who 'pass' this can still have difficulties tracking, i.e. following the words on a page or the writing on the board. Functional vision depends on the maturation of the central nervous system.

Visual-motor integration skills are as important as distance sight. The two eyes have to work together to focus on an image (convergence). Some children with poor convergence will see double images that confuse letter recognition; others will see the letters move on the page and may endure severe eyestrain trying to adjust to the movement. This is Meares-Irlen syndrome, now called visual stress. School-age children can be helped by coloured overlays in books or by having coloured lenses in spectacles. Children also benefit from being allowed to choose the colour of paper that suits them best – different colours defeat reflection of light. Reading books with non-justified print (Barrington Stokes, Edinburgh Publishers) can help too.

Children must also be able to adjust their focus so that they can decipher objects and print from different angles and directions. This is called accommodation. The three skills – convergence, accommodation and tracking – are all prerequisites for quick identification and reading fluently without strain.

The following difficulties and observation points indicate a poor visual sense:

- Poor reading ability due to discrimination or tracking difficulties: play games such as rolling a ball to and from the child to foster tracking.
- Child explaining that letters jump or overlap on the page: visit opticians specialised in colour imaging to see if coloured overlays help.
- Rubbing eyes or partially closing them to keep out the light: check that light sources are not too bright.
- Distress at being asked to read: subtly check all the possibilities mentioned above. Also check hearing as poor sound differentiation may be due to hearing impairment.
- Difficulty following written work on the board: check position of child in relation to board and also tracking skills.
- Handwriting sloping in different directions: check balance and height of the desk and chair. Provide a sloping board. Check/change pencil grip.
- Poor letter formation: try drawing shapes in wet sand. Check pencil grip/change holder.

The auditory sense

During the first three years, the child is listening and learning to tune in to the sounds of his mother tongue, and thereafter it is harder to adjust to the tenor of another language. Obviously, loss of hearing significantly affects learning, but children who 'can hear' may have auditory discrimination problems and these may be the basis of a recognised additional learning need, e.g. dyslexia and dyspraxia. If the child cannot hear the difference between 'p' and 'b' or 'sh' and 'th', then both reading and spelling are impaired. Even silent reading is affected because the child listens to an inner voice. If the sounds are not clear, this process will be affected just the same as in reading aloud.

Hearing too much – i.e. auditory hypersensitivity – can cause as much difficulty as not hearing enough. Children bombarded by sound can have difficulty selecting what they need to hear from the variety of different noises around them. Even in a quiet classroom, some children find hearing the teacher difficult, as they cannot cut out minor rustles and squeaks.

Sounds are transmitted to the language-processing centre in the brain. The right ear is the more efficient. Sounds heard there pass directly to the main language centre in the left hemisphere, whereas left-eared children have to pass the sound to the language subcentre and then through the corpus collosum to the left hemisphere for decoding. This slight delay may put left-eared children at a disadvantage.

The following difficulties and observation points indicate a poor auditory sense:

- Easily distracted: check and cut out extraneous noises such as the humming of a radiator. Be aware of background noises.

- Over-sensitive to sounds: if child holds their hands to their ears, the environment is too noisy. A special programme to stabilise the level of hearing can prevent distortion.
- Poor sense of pitch and tone: practise easy songs and sounds that are high and low. Ask children which is which.
- Confusion in distinguishing letters: check hand dominance after three years.
- Delay in responding/processing: some children need longer to respond. Do not repeat too quickly as this will interrupt the thinking process.
- Not hearing questions clearly which affects responses: check hearing after ensuring that the child is in the best position for listening.
- Constantly asking for words to be repeated: try all the suggestions listed above.

The tactile sense

Tactility or sensitivity to touch is important in feeding, communicating and in generally feeling secure. Touch is one of the earliest sources of learning and touch receptors cover the whole body. They are linked to a headband in the brain – the somatosensory cortex – and it can register heat, cold, pressure, pain and body position. It makes an important contribution to the sense of balance.

Some children have a system that is over-reactive to touch and this causes them to withdraw or be distressed by hugs – responses that most children welcome. This can make them isolated and peers can mistakenly interpret their reactions as snubs. Yet these same children can be 'touchers', seeking out sensory stimulation through contacting others, even though they themselves would be distressed by such overtures.

The pain receptors can cause difficulties, too. Some children are hyposensitive and may not feel pain or temperature change; they may have a huge tolerance to holding hot plates or going out-of-doors ill clad in icy winds. Hyper-sensitive children will over-react about injections and visits to the dentist. Some even feel pain when having their nails or hair cut and some cannot tolerate seams in socks. All kinds of problems arise from being hypo- or hyper-sensitive to touch.

The following difficulties and observation points indicate a poor tactile sense:

- Dislike of being touched so withdraws from contact: firm touch is often tolerated better. Approach child from the front; never startle from behind.
- May be a compulsive toucher: give the child something to hold/squeeze/stroke to keep their hands busy.
- Pain may not be registered appropriately, causing over- or under-reaction: this must be carefully observed. Changes in pallor rather than verbals may indicate pain.
- Poor temperature control: some children feel very hot or cold. Do not insist that they wear extra clothes or prevent them from wearing extra. Their thermostat may be over-sensitive.
- Allergies – possibly eczema: these need medical attention. An epi pen and a practitioner skilled in using it is a must in settings where allergies are present.
- Dislike of contact sports or games: this may be down to fear of being hurt. Use non-contact games or have a soft volleyball rather than a football.
- If the child lacks protective control, they may not sense danger: keep the child away from any potential risk taking.

The senses of smell and taste

The sense of smell is the most evocative of the senses as it can stimulate memories, e.g. of a garden visited long ago or a hot summer when the milk turned sour. The sense of smell can also stimulate the hormones controlling appetite, temperature and sexuality. Certain smells can become associated with different situations, e.g. the smell of a hospital can conjure up memories of pain; the scent of flowers can recall a happy event such as a wedding or a sad one such as a funeral. It is controlled by the thalamus, the part of the brain that relays information between the cortex and the sensory processes.

The sense of taste depends on the sense of smell, so it is not difficult to understand why children often refuse to accept new foods because they do not like the appearance or the smell. Some of the earliest learning comes through these senses, as during the sensory motor period the baby will put everything to the mouth. This most sensitive part of the body will indicate the taste and texture of the object and whether it is hard, soft or malleable as well as whether the taste is pleasant or not.

The senses are not used in isolation but work together to provide a composite picture of events. The study needs to examine each sense, but children with difficulties can learn to depend on one sense to compensate for low acuity in the other.

Q: We are anxious that our three-year-old behaves well when she goes to nursery. At the moment she is strong-willed and often naughty. I'm afraid she won't learn if she doesn't behave.

A: A key strategy in promoting good behaviour is reinforcement. Bandura (1989), a very influential behaviour theorist, acknowledges the influence of biological sources of behaviour but considers that the environment is the major influence in guiding it. A key tenet of his work is that 'behaviour is strengthened by reinforcement'. What does this mean? Well, most children love attention, but if they get more when their behaviour is poor, then that undesirable behaviour is reinforced and they are likely to repeat it, even when the result brings some kind of unpleasantness. It seems that, for many children, being scolded is better than being ignored. This is why parents are advised to ignore poor behaviour, provided it does not incur danger. 'Catch them being good and praise at once' is a wise mantra.

Consistency is important too, for inconsistent responses augur confusion. Even when parents strive to be consistent, things intrude, e.g. a visitor arrives and the child is allowed to watch TV immediately after being naughty just to keep them quiet. This wavering of standards results in unacceptable behaviour becoming 'highly resistant to extinction' in the words of learning theorists.

The major reinforcer is praise given immediately and only when it is honestly won because even at the age of three children evaluate the situation and scorn false praise. Praise is intended to encourage the repetition of desirable behaviours, but even that is not straightforward because the effect on the child is mediated by the respect in which the praise giver is held. As children internalise what has been reinforced, so they develop standards for their own behaviour and ideas about what they should and should not do. So reinforcers are much more that momentary inputs; they contribute to the formation of the child's personality. When children are well behaved at home and at school, the explanation could be that the same kind of behaviour is being reinforced in both settings. Often a child can be pleasant and well mannered in one setting and aggressive and hostile in the other. Researchers would then search for inconsistencies in reinforcement or the clashing effect of different expectations in either setting.

Piaget, studying a few children, intimately focused on internal processes and Bandura concentrated on environmental ones. Different researchers have their own strong beliefs about how the children's personality or self-concept is formed. Both provide insights and ideas for research (see Appendix).

> Q: When I think about learning, I think about intelligence, rather than social learning, but there seem to be doubts as to what this is.

A: Intelligence is much more subtle than being able to get a page of sums correct at school, important though that may be, and over the years many theorists have tried to provide an encompassing definition. Sternberg's theory (1985) is known as the triarchic theory of human intelligence. The first of the three components he calls analytical intelligence and this is what is measured by IQ tests. Planning, organising, remembering facts and applying them in new situations are what make up this component. In small children, signs of intelligence may be bright eyes and a willingness to try new things, remembering where toys are and how they work; attempting to build bricks into a tower; anticipating games; prompting adults to do what they themselves cannot manage; recognising people and other homes. These are skills that show that the children are extending their repertoire of coping strategies in the activities of daily living.

Sternberg calls the second component creative intelligence. This is defined by an ability to see new connections between objects. Those who possess this will question 'conventional wisdom' or what has been accepted by professionals in the field as being true. In young children – perhaps those who set themselves problems and find novel ways of solving them – might be showing some imaginative response or the first signs of creative intelligence. In the early years, however, the term 'imaginative' would be more fitting because 'creativity' suggests that whatever is produced can stand scrutiny by an expert in the field and youngsters do not have the experience to meet this criterion. However, it is important that children have many opportunities to nurture their imagination and creative potential because 'the seeds of great things could be sown at a young age' (Dixon 2005).

The third component is called practical intelligence. Sometimes children with this capacity are called 'streetwise'. They can look after their own interests and cope when others would tumble. Three-year-old Jay is a case in point. He would play happily, unsupervised in the street. When a car intending to park approached, he would sit down on the kerb, place his Wellington-clad feet in the gutter and refuse to move. So he protected his space – until Social Services discovered his ploy. However, he had worked out how to get what he wanted, for no one dared lift him to move him on.

Sternberg's claim was not just that **intelligence quotient** (IQ) tests only measured his first type, i.e. analytic intelligence, but that the other types might be more useful in the hurly-burly of coping with life. Elaborating on the idea that there were several types of intelligence, Gardner (1983) named seven. This was instrumental in making educationalists appreciate the wider scope of intelligence and help curriculum planners give equal importance to subjects that had been viewed in some regions as peripheral. The seven different kinds he identified as follows.

Linguistic: the ability to use language effectively. Certainly, the timing of when babies start to babble and then use words is a key measure of this ability (see the development of language on p. 88).

Logical/mathematical: this describes an ease and competence with numbers. Toddlers could be showing this if they line up bricks in size order; make patterns with necklaces; are fascinated by number songs and understand that five buns (in the baker's shop) are more than four; can set the table for a doll's tea party with the correct number of plates (showing they have understood one-to-one correspondence); understand about siphons in the water tray.

Musical: the ability to appreciate music. Many toddlers dance happily to their favourite tunes. Some can sing in tune before they can speak. Some have a good sense of rhythm and enjoy nursery rhymes, often getting much pleasure from supplying the rhyming word. Providing opportunities to play instruments and hear music is very important for its own sake and because the old adage, 'musicians are good at maths' is being proved true. Winkley (2004) showed that 'each fingertip is connected to a large piece of tissue in the frontal cortex of the brain and as this is the region for problem solving or executive function, fingertip activities stimulate the area critically important for learning'.

Spatial: the ability to appreciate relationships and what they mean, e.g. in a work of art. Young children who show proportion in their drawings of people or objects may have this capability. Another example would be children who look for the spaces on a games field, i.e. who are tactically aware in games or who remember the way home. Older children will be able to follow or draw a map and find their way through crowds to their destination.

The Goodenough (1972) 'Draw a Man' test is a good way to find out how children of 2½–7 years perceive spatial/body relationships. The children are asked to draw a man (this is something within every child's experience) and they are given a point for every detail they put in. It doesn't matter if arms come out of balloon-shaped bodies. If they are drawn they score a point; similarly, for hands and toes and facial details such as eyebrows and teeth. This is a highly revealing test, still used in many psychological assessments.

Bodily kinaesthetic: the ability to move in a co-ordinated, fluent way with minimal waste of energy. High-level athletes and sports people possess this kind of intelligence in droves. In children, those who walk early, who climb and try to jump and who do not bump into furniture or fall over thin air may have this type of intelligence. They need daily opportunities to develop the ability, e.g. playing at the swing park, crawling up stairs or finding their way round an obstacle course.

Figure 5.3 A group of 'musicians' playing and singing together. They are learning about co-operation, developing their sense of rhythm and their listening skills

Interpersonal intelligence: the ability to be sensitive to the needs of others; to have well-developed altruism and empathy. Young children who have this kind of intelligence will offer a pat of comfort to a distressed mother; sense when to be quiet; try to help; play with the child who always gets left out, have this kind of intelligence.

Intrapersonal: the ability to understand oneself. This self-knowledge is a basis or starter for understanding other people and making comparisons and assessments. It is an important part of the self-concept. Think of children choosing friends. In the early days, mothers probably chose suitable children; slightly older children are likely to choose people who have the same interests. Increasingly, however, as they mature they may identify in others the skills they wish they had and wish to be friends with them. These others may not be the ones the parents would choose and this can be a source of real conflict.

In his book *Five Minds for the Future*, Gardner (2007) makes us think of how we can encourage children to develop these intellectual/social/motor/emotional competences. The skills that youngsters will need to contribute to their future are named by Gardner as follows.

* A disciplined mind, for it is important that children can focus and achieve mastery in one or more disciplines.
* One that can synthesize, i.e. sift information and select what is pertinent.
* One that is creative, so that children can think beyond the ordinary and mundane.
* One that is respectful, so that children value diversity and difference.
* One that is ethical, for this lets children tell the truth.

It is probably unreal to expect a three-year-old to have a disciplined mind (in adult terms), but if this is a critical competence perhaps we should think of promoting it for this age group? One of the benefits of play is that children can try out several activities and abandon those that don't suit them. Some children will flit around and really not stay long enough to derive any benefit. Perhaps, after some free play, limiting the choice and encouraging children who wander or flit to complete a jigsaw or a painting or whatever, could urge them towards meeting this first criterion. Could this ensure more concentration and lead to new discoveries?

The second criterion may be stimulated by giving children choices and asking them to explain why they made that choice. This would make the activity purposeful and could raise its value in the children's eyes. This would contribute to the first criterion as well.

The third could be stimulated by giving unusual resources and letting the children's imagination have free rein. It is important that adults do not limit the children by their own view of what things are for or how things should be done. This is much more difficult than teaching them to make something, but it would help children to think beyond the mundane.

Perhaps the last two criteria could be modelled by staff. The children would then see how they interacted, so that respect for children, their parents and their work is the order of the day. Taking time to listen is so important and giving children full attention, even for a brief spell, shares the message that they, their family and their work are valued. How important is that? This new thinking houses many ideas for further exploration and research. Questions such as, 'How can I promote (whatever is the aim)?', 'What changes do I need to make? And when I do, to what extent does this enable two or three children (name them) to achieve (whatever the aim was)?'

> Q: Harry, a foster father was worried by his child's ability to lie with conviction. 'He looks us straight in the eye and has us fooled into believing his stories. He's just three and I don't suppose he understands what telling lies means, but will he become a pathological liar? How would we cope with that?'

A: Harry may be surprised to find that 'the ability to tell fibs at two and three is the sign of a fast developing brain'. Researchers at Toronto University directed by Dr Kang Lee (2010) claim that 'children who fib show better intellectual development because they can cover up their tracks'. Dr Lee explains that lying involves multiple brain processes such as integrating various sources of information and manipulating the data to their advantage. This is linked to the development of regions of the brain that allow executive functioning. It was also a skill recommended in *Five Minds for the Future* (Gardner 2007). The team went on to calm Harry's fears about long-term lying by explaining that 50 per cent of three-year-olds tell lies and that there 'is no link between childhood fibs and becoming cheats or fraudsters later in life'. In fact, they claim that 'little liars grow up to be great leaders'.

So educationalists must still explore the ways in which children learn, because only then can they match and time their input in the most appropriate way. Sometimes they must have the courage to stay in the background to give children space to develop their ideas and ploys, for who knows what they may discover?

Chapter 6

The development of language

The development of language is a huge milestone for parents and babies as it augments the non-verbal communication that has been a key in both bonding, interpreting the babies' needs and reciprocating in games such as Peek-a-boo. Beginning to speak at the correct time also reassures that development is on track. In the development of language, just as in other competences, there are wide 'normal times' for achieving language, for some babies speak early while others wait longer, but catch up quickly and even overtake those who made a precocious start. Some babies who have had all their needs met without speaking may not feel the need. As in everything else, babies have an inbuilt timetable that usually responds to encouragement and opportunity, but despite this, some babies prefer to wait. It is also wise for adults to remember that to speak, babies must learn to control 150 muscles in their lips, their soft palate and tongue, and this strength and control can take time to mature. But from the babies' facial expressions and non-verbal responses, parents and carers can deduce if their child understands what is being said. This is a very important assessment, for non-verbal communication carries 90 per cent of the message in any interaction. If you doubt this, try describing a circle or, if this is easy, a spiral without using your hands. If babies obviously understand, parents can relax, secure in the knowledge that their 'babies are hardwired to learn language' (Winston 2004: 83). This is shown even before birth when kicks and squirms in utero quieten, seeming to indicate that babies are listening to their mother's voice.

In 90–95 per cent of people, the language cortex is situated in the left hemisphere of the brain, generally corresponding to those who are right-handed (Carter 2000). Right-handedness is strongly associated with left-brain dominance and in these people the organising, systematising area is stronger than the right side – the more creative side. Although both **hemispheres** are involved in all tasks, one side is said to be dominant. Anecdotally, left-handers are thought to be artistic and imaginative because they are right-brain dominant. Left-handed people are also slightly different in the way their brains are organised. This explains why no one should attempt to change a child's preferred hand, which was a common practice in the past. However, about 70 per cent of left-handers still have their language centres in the left hemisphere and the other 30 per cent have them in both hemispheres. Handedness is well established before babies are born. In fact, some babies can be seen sucking their preferred thumbs at 15 weeks' gestation. Other children will still be ambivalent about their choice of preferred hand at three years of age. This can be seen when they paint with one hand one day and the other the next. But when they are three or four, staff can help them achieve hand dominance by sharing games, e.g. throwing bean bags into a pail and pointing out which hand got the best score or catching ping-pong balls rolled down

Figure 6.1 Leah is finding which hand gets the best score, so establishing a sense of hand dominance. Observe her floppy wrist and the effort shown by her protruding tongue. Perhaps this general lack of strength explains her delay in achieving hand dominance

corrugated cardboard. Knowing and using the preferred hand or foot can ease writing and aiming tasks, while not being sure can cause confusion – even in picking up a pencil – and delay in completing every task.

The two main speech areas in the brain are known as Wernicke's area and Broca's area, and these have been identified for some considerable time. When proper language begins generally at the start of the second year, it shows that these two areas have been activated. Wernicke's area is responsible for comprehension while Broca's area generates speech (articulation) and may contain a grammar module (Carter 2000: 226). Children are always tested for comprehension as well as for clarity of articulation and the number of words they speak because this shows that both areas are functioning. This is very important because some children display a wide vocabulary without much understanding of the words that are spoken. This is called hyperlexia. Often a large vocabulary can be considered a sign of intelligence, but not if the child does not appreciate what the words mean. Not appreciating the meaning can lead to out-of-context speech, as seen in autism and **Williams syndrome**.

Recent brain imaging studies show that other areas beyond the left hemisphere are involved in producing language. A recent 'being tested' idea is that there is a language area in the **cerebellum**, the area at the back of the brain that is primarily involved in muscle tone, in motor control and in relaying incoming sensory impulses to the correct area in the brain for interpretation. The possibility of a language centre there could help to explain the link between dyslexia and dyspraxia, for 50 per cent of children who have one of those specific learning difficulties have the other (Kirby 1999).

So what do parents and practitioners want to know about the language development of their children?

Q: Are the babbles and other sounds babies make really a form of language?

A: Generally, these very early sounds are not referred to as language per se, as they are not used to refer to things or events. They do stimulate communication and offer opportunities for practice but the sounds are not used as symbols, they do not stand for something else. It is the use of symbols that delineates progress from one stage of development to the next and this should be carefully recorded for assessment. The babbles are useful in that they are pleasing communications but, generally speaking, it is the parents and carers who infer meaning from the early exchange of sounds. However, if the same sound is used consistently in conjunction with an object, this sound could be described as language. For several weeks my own daughter had us mystified by her excitement at seeing a 'boonger'. 'See a boonger' was an oft repeated request whenever we went for a walk. Eventually, by a process of elimination, we discovered it was a dog on a lead. Now despite this being nonsensical, it could be called language because the word consistently referred to the same thing. Luckily, this phase passed as real words took over.

Q: I've heard of 'joint attention' in relation to babies' developing language. What's that?

A: Joint attention describes another early stage in language development. When this happens, the adult and child together pay attention to a particular object or happening, and they share their interest by gestures, by holding gaze, by pointing or by exclaiming. Often the adult will name the object and the child will listen and try to name it, too. Or, if an event is described, 'Oh good, Dad has made some tea and is putting toast on your tray', then the beginning of the sequencing of events is shared. As this interaction happens, the duo will be involved in turn-taking and they will highlight the meaning in the interaction. In this way, the child, even pre-speech, is developing skills that are essential to using language that is contextually sound. Shared meaning and reciprocity are being laid down as precursors of more sophisticated conversations.

An example will help to explain joint attention. The baby has some pudding and then burps. Mother holds the gaze and asks, 'You really enjoyed that, didn't you?', probably nodding at the same time. So the burp and the nod become part of a conversation. This leads to joint attention and the mutual understanding of gestures. At six months, a baby will follow a mother's gaze to see what she is noticing, even without her specifically pointing, and by nine or ten months the baby, through pointing and possibly making urgent hard-to-ignore sounds, will direct the mother's gaze to what is important.

Non-verbally, the baby is saying 'Look at this' and the mother will obey and probably extend the interaction. 'Oh yes, that's a blue ball, a blue ball. That's your blue ball' and then, offering it to the baby, ask, 'Would you like to hold it?' This repetition helps listening skills and extends the child's repertoire of naming words. These phrases tend to be said rhythmically and babies' ears seem tuned to appreciate the cadence of the sentences, so the exchange, which might sound strange to the outsider, is a shared communication that is pleasing to both mother and baby. This reinforces bonding, **attachment** and learning.

So joint attention is very important. With turn-taking, it sets the tone for later dialogues. In these shared episodes, the child is developing skills that are essential to speaking, to understanding language and to the mastery of grammar. Another version of honing these skills comes a little later in reading storybooks together. A good idea is to have pauses for pointing to pictures and repeating names and ideas, e.g. 'Where is the dog? Is he thirsty, do you think? What does he need?' These extensions help to extend thinking beyond the actual words on the page.

Q: You say that babies are wired to learn language. That's the nature or innate part, but what about the nurture part? How important is the environment?

A: Babies are born with, or soon develop, the ability to discriminate speech sounds and by one or two months they can tell the difference between different sounds. Babies are also very sensitive to the rhythm of sounds and, from the earliest days, they are intrigued by the stress and intonation that is the rhythm of words. This is why an environment rich in words is critically important. Huttenlocher (1998) has shown that the frequency with which parents speak to their children up to the age of two has major implications for their language use throughout the rest of their lives, proving that this is a critical time for learning language.

Language comes naturally to children provided they hear it during infancy. However, if they are deprived of language sounds their brains may become physically disordered. (Carter 2000: 256) Carter tells of one child who had been shut away. She was only discovered when she was 13. With extensive coaching she did learn some words, but she could not master the grammar. These two things normally develop together. Brain imaging found that due to non-use, her language area had atrophied and the spoken words she did produce came from a different area of her brain. The critical time for learning language had been missed, making it extremely difficult or impossible for the girl to catch up. The timing of input to language learning as in all other forms is critical.

Hollich (2000) makes an important claim. He explains that the ways in which mothers and other adults speak to their babies enforces the process by which they learn the specific phonemes of their own language.

Q: Does this mean there are different ways? Can babies really distinguish between them? Is one better than the other?

A: In her article, 'Bright as a new newborn baby,' Marjorie Wallace from SANE created an impact in her opening lines. She wrote that you can forget about 'itchy coo'. Babies are in danger of being bored to tears by our childish approach to them.' Obviously, she agrees with Hollich (2000) who is sure that babies know much more than we give them credit for. For them, baby talk is a no-no.

Yet others advise that 'Babies learn best from melodic, over-exaggerated gentle conversations; when this happens they learn about cadences and rhythms and rhymes and have time to internalize the sounds of their own language' (BBC 2005).

Many adults instinctively communicate with babies using what would seem to be nonsense phrases such as 'helloooo ickle baba'. But in some cultures children are never exposed to this kind of interaction and yet both sets of children learn to talk. Perhaps some adults are more expressive and relaxed with babies than others. The exaggerated rhythm, however, does seem to be enjoyed, holding the baby's attention for longer and producing responsive gurgles and smiles.

However, with conflicting advice from sources like this and, of course, from the experiences of grandmothers, how are new parents, carers and practitioners to know what is the best way to interact with the very young children in their care? Most developmental psychologists agree that the simplified rhythmical language in a higher pitch that mothers almost instinctively speak to their babies is very helpful. This is called **motherese** or, more recently, **infant-directed speech**. Here, short sentences are repeated using simple vocabulary and most often with reinforcement (repetition) or recasting, i.e. taking the sentence into new pastures. So if the baby exclaims 'want tat', mother would possibly reply, 'That's your red hat. Your red hat will keep you cosy-posy today. Let's put on your red hat.' This done, holding the child to the mirror to see. 'Don't you look smart wearing your cosy red hat? It will keep you as warm as toast.' Winston (2004) claims that children *prefer* to listen to motherese, 'the short musical tones encourage the children to listen more' and in recasting, i.e. repeating their words with add-ons, they learn new ideas and hear more words.

Recasting has additional values. First, researchers found that babies could differentiate between infant-directed (ID) speech and other kinds and that they preferred or paid more attention to their own (ID) kind (Snow 1997). But in addition, the recasting of the babies' own utterances resulted in their being more able to pick up the correct grammatical form. This 'following the child philosophy' is proving to be as important in language development as it is in play and other kinds of intellectual learning.

Q: When adults interact with babies, are there other differences beyond the kind of words they use?

A: Bee and Boyd (2005) have collected data of the process of adult–infant interaction and found that there are other kinds of differences, as you say. They found that when adults engage a baby, they stay much closer to them than they would to another adult. They use a higher pitch, a great deal of repetition and more gestures. Unfortunately, some adults will do this with disabled youngsters who have passed well beyond this stage. This causes mortification and hurt, and shows that not all adults have developed the sensitivity that should underlie positive interactions.

Some of the early researchers claimed that children learned language skills because adults reinforced the correct usage and this led to internalisation and imitation. This seemed entirely plausible. If children speak in similar ways to the adults around them and have the same dialect, how else could that be? The environment must play a major part in influencing the child's acquisition of language. Messer (1994), however, found that although adults stressed the important words in communication and corrected any naming mistakes such as 'That's a cow' when the child had called it a dog, they did not correct grammatical errors. This supported Pinker's (1994) hypothesis in his book, *The Language Instinct*, that 'complex language is universal because children actually invent it – generation after generation, not because they are taught, not because they are generally smart, not because it is useful to them but because they just can't help it'.

> Q: Do babies learn best if they hear stories, even at an early age?

A: Developmentalists now know that babies who hear lots of language, be it in conversations or stories, develop larger vocabularies, use more complex sentences and learn to read more easily once they go to school (Snow 1997). One group of researchers, (Whitehurst *et al.* 1998) encouraged parents and practitioners to read stories using what they called '**dialogic reading**'. They had to intersperse questions that could not be answered by pointing and required some deduction on the part of the child. So, looking at a picture of a sunny day, parents might ask, 'Would this be a good day to do a big washing, do you think?' or 'I wonder what will happen to the little red hen if he eats all the bread by himself?' At the end of the research (which was replicated in other countries) children who had participated in the dialogic reading scheme were found to have enhanced vocabularies and better grammar. Moreover, this effect lasted through their childhood (Bee and Boyd 2005). This would fulfil the EYPS status criterion S16, 'engage in shared sustained thinking with children'.

So in the time before children begin to read for themselves, storytelling is a happy, shared experience and a valuable precursor for later reading. Adult and child develop a shared empathy for the characters in the story and can discuss ways of resolving problems. Long before reading has been thought about, children can relish the adventures of the three pigs and empathise with the poor pig that built his house of straw.

> Q: Should babies only hear their native language or is it a good idea to try to make them bilingual?

A: At birth we are all international, i.e. we could learn any language, but very soon this capacity disappears. Even at five or six months the babbling sounds of French or Japanese babies are very different because they are only using the set of phonemes they have heard. By less than a year old babies only relate to the set of sounds particular to their own tongue (Winston 2004). Yet children going to a nursery at age three or so, where only a different language is spoken, can amaze us by the speed at which they learn a second language and at first sight being bilingual may seem a huge advantage. However, there are pros and cons, depending on whether the home is bilingual. Where it is, parents are encouraged to give equal time for speaking and listening to both languages.

In preschool and junior classes, being bilingual helps children think about the composition of their languages. This skill is called metalinguistic ability. They also focus better on language tasks. On the down side, however, many bilingual children reach some milestones later than their monolingual peers. Their vocabularies are as large, but divided between the two languages. When their schooling is conducted in the language in which they are less fluent, some learning problems may emerge. In the long run, being bilingual is certainly advantageous because adult learners of a second language never quite have the same degree of fluency or the same accent. 'We develop our first language and learn others' (Winston 2004: 270) and in so doing we fail to master some sounds and will always have an accent that leaves us exposed as a non-native speaker. Japanese adults cannot master 'l' and 'r' because these sounds are not used in that language, and some English speakers, born only a few miles from the Trossachs, cannot master the 'ch' of Loch Lomond. They talk about 'Lock' Lomond when they take the high or the low road. Second languages are processed in a different section of the language area to the mother tongue. This is why people who have a stroke may forget their first language, yet still be able to speak in their second, even in one they didn't know they possessed.

Q: Is there a timetable for the earliest months?

A: From birth to about a month old, the baby only makes a crying sound. However, these become increasingly expressive, signalling the baby's needs, e.g. hunger, pain or needing to be changed or simply wanting to be picked up. At about two months the baby will experiment with more sounds. This stage, when babies will listen to their own vowel sounds 'oooooo', making them softer and louder, is called '**cooing**.' Then consonants appear at about seven months when the baby gains the muscle strength to combine vowels and consonants. This is the start of babbling. 'Babbling' is a word that describes strings of repetitive sounds, e.g. 'dadadadada' or 'babababababa' and these strings will develop the intonation of sentences. Adults repeat them back to babies and this is an early 'conversation' than gives much pleasure and reasurrance to both parties.

At ten months or so babies develop their gestures, e.g. pointing, opening and closing their fist as if to say 'Bring me that', and the meaning is quite clear. At the same time games with gestures are enjoyed, e.g. 'pat-a-cake' or 'round and round the garden'. Babies love endless repetition and anticipate the endings, e.g. 'a tickly under there' long before they happen. This shows their memories are working well.

Babies can understand much more than they can say. This is **receptive language** and mothers find that their babies at 10 months can understand about 30 words and at 13 months they understood about 100 words (Fenson 1994). This shows that the 9–10-month time is when babies combine gestures and sounds, the time for babbling the first language sounds, the first joining in gesture games, the first understanding of single words. The first real words appear at about one year.

Q: My one-year-old makes up her own words. For example, when she wants a drink, she calls out 'nenenene'. When we go in the car, she points to houses and says the same sounds. Is that OK and why does she do that?

A: It's perfectly all right. The baby's comprehension is ahead of her ability to form words. Regarding the claim that early sounds are not really words, Bates *et al.* (1988) explain that, in their view, sounds can be considered as words if the child uses them consistently in the presence of an object. So, adults should enjoy the sounds and write them down so that they can smile together when the child is older. Some families even retain early attempts at difficult words their children have produced, e.g. 'workle bokl' for hot-water bottle, and they remain a source of reminiscence and smiles for years.

Q: Are there developmental norms for language?

A: Yes, as in all other important competences there are age lists. These are given in the following chart.

Table 6.1 A summary chart for the development of speech

Age	Words	A developmental plan for speaking Stories	Activities
5 years	Clear articulation; compound phrases.	Can retell a story; suggest new ideas. Can sequence three pictures. Uses pronouns now. May read single words. Likes to have scribing of own ideas done.	Can empathise with others' feelings; understands rules and routines. Looks for a friend and will co-operate in a game.
4 years	Seeks explanations. Asks 'When?' 'Why?' Can visualise events elsewhere.	Enjoys repetition and contributing known phrases to stories. Can retell a story or invent one.	Can role play. Can understand characterisation. Plays a ball game with a friend.

Table 6.1 continued

Age	Words	A developmental plan for speaking Stories	Activities
3 years	Uses sentences of 4–5 words. Complex use of words.	Will listen, adapt and recast sentences. Uses 'Why?' constantly. Plays with nonsense words and rhymes.	Joins in songs and rhymes. Beats rhythms. Enjoys drawing with coloured chalks.
2 years	Huge increase in vocabulary – the naming explosion. Links two words, e.g. 'love you', 'go away'.	Follows stories – recognises favourite characters and routines. Gesture and body language combined – holophrases. Communication strategies used, e.g. motherese (higher pitched simplified language).	Asserts independence – has tantrums. Telegraphic speech, i.e. uses only essential words, e.g. 'I going'.
1 year	Monosyllabic babbling – 'da, da, da'. Understanding evident from facial expression and gestures.	Understands simple instructions, e.g. 'come here'. Can convey wishes through gestures. Understands 50 words. Makes own words for wants. Words learned slowly at this pre-linguistic stage.	Enjoys peek-a-boo (the basis of turn taking). Memory and a sense of self is developing.
3–9 months	Controls gestures. Joint attention beginning to develop.	Beginning to understand several words. Babbling 'dadadada' on request at 9+ months.	Uses smiling to good effect. Claps hands; beginning to point.
Birth –3 months	Cries, increasingly with meaning.	Beginning to communicate with gurgles. Coo-ing.	Recognises familiar people as source of comfort.

So yes, there are timetables but to begin with, learning words is a very slow process. In the first six months of using words, vocabulary only increases to about 30 words. Separate words are used in specific contexts for at this stage the toddler has not grasped that words are symbolic, i.e. that they refer to objects outwith the context.

By 16–24 months children add words very quickly. This is sometimes called the naming explosion (Bee and Boyd: 2005: 213). A 16-month-old speaks about 50 words and by age two the child has 320 words, including 'No'. These come in a spurt. Questions beginning 'But why?' abound, and from then on a moment of quiet is golden time.

Q: What about the older ones? When should they string words together?

A: At 2½ children have 600 words and most parents have given up counting. By 5 or 6 the vocabulary has risen to 15,000 words. When they begin to put sentences together, generally they are short, e.g. 'I tired' or 'I not want it'. At this stage children have rules for their sentences that differ from adult rules. After all, if 'I wanted. . .' is correct, why is 'I wented' wrong? Adding 'ed' to everything to make the past tense is very common. Interestingly, gifted and talented children go through this phase very quickly; their correct grammar is often one early sign of their gift.

Gradually, sentences get longer. By 24 months children use four- and five-word sentences; by 30 months that has doubled. This is linked to the size of vocabularies the children have. By the time they are three, children are able to combine two ideas into complex sentences, e.g.: these flowers are snowdrops, aren't they? The really enormous progress is between one and four as the child moves from single words to complex questions, negatives and commands, such as 'Do this *now*'.

> Q: What about deaf children? How do they learn to speak?

A: Winston (2004: 112) explains that 'you do not need to be able to hear to develop language' and that MRI scans of deaf children born to deaf parents who grew up using signing, have a language area as well developed as non-deaf children. Interestingly, hearing children never seem to develop the facility in signing that deaf children do. They use a broken version of signing, just like foreign adults trying to learn English.

> Q: What about speech impediments, such as stuttering? Why should children do this?

A: Carter (2000) explains that children who stutter have different patterns of brain activity. Their right hemispheres are more active than in other children, so stuttering may be due to competition for dominance between the hemispheres. Both sides try to produce sounds with the double sounds emerging. There is also a difference in the way they hear their own voice due to their auditory loop being underactive. When children read aloud with others their stutter disappears because they are receiving the auditory feedback from the other children. To support them, it is essential to keep distracting sounds in the environment to a minimum and to keep the atmosphere calm by listening carefully and not asking the child to repeat words that have proved difficult.

> Q: What about children with autism? I've heard about disappearing speech being a sign of autism. It is so frightening to think that could happen.

A: Some children who babble and even say one or two words may lose this ability at around 2½ and this can be one of the early signs of autism. However, the range of language skills within autism is wide; some children with Asperger's syndrome at the high functioning end of the spectrum have prolific speech, even if it is pedantic and tends to lack intonation. The fundamental problem is poor communication due to inappropriate speech. If a child makes a verbal overture but gets a baffling response or no response or one they don't understand, they will be mystified and unlikely to repeat their request. If this pattern happens regularly, the confused child withdraws or shuts down. The normal pattern where communication precedes language is disrupted in children with autism and they miss the socialisation process that indicates what to say and when to say it. Mainstream schools tend to assume that the early skills of communication such as joint attention have been mastered but in children on the autistic spectrum, this is not so. For them, and possibly other children, gestures and facial expressions can be meaningless and at worst, turn their world into 'a silent terrifying place where nothing makes sense' (Jane Asher, President of the Autistic Society).

So there are many ways for parents and practitioners to support their children through communicating calmly and sharing ideas as well as reading stories, enjoying rhymes and listening to what they say. In so doing parents can be sure that they are building on the inbuilt competences their children have; they have fostered a critically important skill and hopefully they have found the process enjoyable as well as being so worthwhile, for through these activities they are building enduring, worthwhile relationships as well as enhancing language and learning.

The next question was asked by a group of practitioners who were recording the interactions of three-year-old children. They had found the terminology difficult.

> Q: The language of developing speech is complex and confusing for us, yet we need to understand the differences. Can you help?

A: There are four main parts to language competence. Let's try to explain the terms.

- First there is phonology – this describes the rules of sounds.
- Then there is syntax. This describes the grammatical rules that govern speech.
- Semantics is the term used to describe the meaning conveyed by speech.
- Pragmatics concerns the social context that influences the kind of speech that is used.

Phonology is the system that decides the particular sounds (or phonemes) used in the child's community. The 'ch' in the Scottish name for loch that many non-Scots pronounce as lock is an example of local use of phonemes, as is the Welsh use of 'll' that defeats many non-Welsh speakers.

Syntax describes the way in which words are used to make grammatical sentences. Most children naturally progress through two-word utterances 'Jake bikit' to 'Please can I have a biscuit?' (Some children will not use the personal pronoun 'I' and this should be carefully monitored with dates and ages recorded as it may show an underlying problem.)

Semantics refers to the meaning of words. To make sense, phonemes must be combined to make morphemes, the smallest meaningful parts of language. Children go through the stage of adding 'ed' to many words to signify the past tense, e.g. 'I go-ed to bed', but this passes quite quickly as a more adult form of speech is learned. One four-year-old, looking over Arthur's Seat, an extinct volcano in Edinburgh, proudly and loudly announced, 'That hill is stinkered'. It took the bemused adults a moment to recognise what he meant.

Pragmatics is the understanding that the same words can mean different things in different contexts and that truthful utterances are not always helpful or kind. Gradually, children learn when to whisper or wait to ask questions if they have the potential to hurt or dismay. Children with autism can find this extraordinarily difficult and so unwittingly cause offence in public places. This competence depends on developing empathy and altruism, i.e. understanding that others may be hurt by truths. Most children will have developed this by age four or so.

So understanding how children come to be skilled communicators is difficult but it makes a fascinating study. Why do some develop two languages, one for the playground and another for school? The fact that they do shows how much the context influences children's choice of words. How do they instinctively know that certain words and phrases in certain places are taboo?

Summary

Explaining how children learn language has proved to be one of the most difficult challenges within developmental psychology. 'There is a veritable chasm between what the children hear and how they create sentences of their own' (Pinker 1987). The amount and variety of speech sounds and languages children hear is significant. The difference between children who are disadvantaged in terms of being listened to and read to leads to them having a language gap at age four and this gap widens over the school years. The disadvantaged children don't catch up. Again, this points to the notion of critical learning times when the brain is 'ready' to absorb specific kinds of information. So the richness and variety of the language children hear in the first one, two or three years is critically important in determining their progress.

Debates over the importance of motherese or infant-directed speech vary, too. Studies of children in other cultures where there is no such thing also learn language. So although it is helpful, it cannot be claimed to be essential. The group of innate theorists, e.g. Dan Slobin, assert that every child is born with a basic language made up of a set of operating principles. Children, they explain, are innate linguists, who spontaneously apply their developing understanding to language. From the earliest days they are searching for patterns and regularities to develop their speech.

In contrast, the constructivist group of theorists claim that what is important is not the built-in or innate biases, but the children's construction of language as part of the broader picture of intellectual development. They argue that from the beginning, children set out to communicate, and this they do with gestures and sounds and later words. The children learn new words when they are necessary to communicate their thoughts and feelings. Supporting this is the link between children's play with objects as symbols. Children will use an empty cup to feed a toy at about a year, which is the time when they speak their first word. Children who have delayed language very often have delayed imaginative or symbolic play as well. Children who show advanced symbolic play, perhaps combining a series of gestures such as rocking a doll, feeding it and then patting its back are likely to be advanced in their language development as well (McCune 1995).

So although much has been discovered about the development of children's language, Bee and Boyd (2005) show that there are no theorists who 'have cracked the code' and 'the fact that children learn the complex and varied use of their native tongue remains both miraculous and largely mysterious'.

Conclusion

Magical and mysterious could be descriptors of the intricacies of observing and assessing children's development and finding that each child brings an individual and enthralling addition to the wisdom of previous authors and researchers. This means that the search for new understandings must go on and on. I hope the text has given you ideas and clarified some things that may have been perplexed you, and that you will be anxious to try out some research in your own setting.

Parents, carers and professionals reflecting on their previous encounters with young children will wonder how well all their careful input has nurtured the children in their care, and I hope that reading the text will have provided insights to give confidence and strategies to evaluate progress across the different aspects of development. Perhaps, reflecting on earlier interactions, you will wonder whether a different approach might have been more beneficial?

'But how are you to know?' I hear you ask. As the book shows, the children themselves play a huge part in their own development and what 'works' with one, fazes another. This is because each brings their own set of aptitudes and attitudes, and these are based on their own cultural and social context. It is difficult to get it right all of the time, but with experience and commitment and, I hope, pleasure, we shall.

Parents, carers and professionals aim to nurture each aspect of the children's development in the most conducive environment so that the children learn to walk and run, speak and play, and find joy in all these achievements. Like development itself, the learning path has bumps, but then, as adults we realise that 'you have to go through the rain to appreciate the sunshine'. When empathy goes hand in hand with guidance, the sun shines and the child is fortunate indeed. Nothing is more important than giving each child the best start that we can for, after all, 'it is to the young that the future belongs'.

Appendix

Potential topics for study

This list gives ideas that professionals will find helpful in choosing areas for study. From years of helping student teachers to find topics for their research projects, I realised that at the start they found it difficult to decide on a topic, but examples clarified their thinking.

Some ways of honing these down to find research questions are suggested, but these have to be contextualised to match the children and the setting. The process is fully explained in my book *The Art of Action Research in the Classroom*. The word 'classroom' is meant to cover any learning experience – home or nursery or school.

1   When should children be allowed to take risks? How can we build a safe environment yet one that has the potential for challenges?
2   What are children learning as they play out of doors, in any area?
3   How can I encourage a lone child to become more social?
4   What is the best way to develop a relationship with the parents of a four-year-old boy who appears to be globally delayed? I have found language strategies that I could share with his parents but they are reluctant to admit there is anything wrong. They say he speaks at home.
5   How can I teach a child to crawl using the cross-lateral pattern? What are the implications if the child does not crawl?
6   How do I monitor a child who is extremely bright and does not match any of the tables on developmental norms?
7   Why are two children in the same family so different in their abilities and attitudes?
8   When does a child realise that they are either a boy or a girl? What can I do to avoid gender bias in my setting?

You can take any topic that interests you, focus on a specific part, then clarify exactly what you want to discover through asking the following questions:

What is it I want to find out?
What action (s) will I take to gather evidence?
How will I record my findings?
What texts, books, papers will provide a starting ground?
How can I assure parents of confidentiality?

Do try and good luck!

Glossary

Glossary terms in the text are emboldened at their first mention.

Accommodation The part of the adaptation process by which a child modifies existing schemas to fit new experiences. A Piagetan concept.

Affectational bond An enduring tie: a special relationship formed in the process of growing up.

Afferent Information leading to the brain.

Amnion The sac in which the foetus grows during prenatal life.

Amygdala An almond-shaped structure involved in emotional function, fear conditioning, and the storing of emotional memories.

Apgar score An assessment chart for newborns measuring heart and breathing rates, muscle tone, movement and responsiveness.

Assimilation Part of the learning experience that involves adding information to existing schemas. These are modified to fit pre-existing schemas.

Attachment A strong bond providing a stable base and a sense of security, and housing a set of instinctive communicative behaviours, e.g. smiling, holding eye contact.

Authoritarian parental style One of three modes showing high levels of control and low levels of nurturance and maturity demands.

Authoritative parental style One of the three modes showing high levels of nurturance, communication and maturity demands.

Autism A condition characterised by three key symptoms: very poor social interaction; failure to understand non-verbal communication and the emotions of others; pedantic, out-of-context speech, very limited speech or, in severe cases, no speech at all.

Axon The long dendrite extending from the neuron. Its terminal fibres make synaptic connections with dendrites of other neurons.

Babbling The repetitive sounds made by a baby from around six to twelve months of age.

Blastocyst The mass of cells that begin to subdivide at four days after conception. The mass forms a hollow sphere with two layers of cells around the perimeter. The outer layer will form the support structures while the inner layer forms the embryo itself.

Brain stem The part of the brain emerging from the spinal cord and connected to the cerebral hemispheres. It has three parts: the midbrain, pons and medulla oblongata. It regulates the basic functions of the body that are essential for survival, such as breathing, blood pressure and control of the heart rate.

Caesarean section Delivery of the baby through an incision in the mother's abdomen rather than vaginally.

Central nervous system The brain. The spinal cord and optic nerves are part of this controlling system. It joins the peripheral nervous system that is made of afferent nerves carrying impulses from the body to the brain and efferent nerves that take motor impulses to the muscles.

Cephalocaudal development One of the two basic processes in physical development (the other is proximodistal) that describes the increase in bodily strength moving from head to toe. Thus, babies can hold their heads up before they sit and sit before they stand.

Cerebellum The structure above and to the back of the brain stem responsible for muscle tone, and sifting and relaying incoming 'instructions' to the correct part of the cortex for analysis.

Cerebro-spinal fluid Fluid surrounding the brain and spinal cord. Containing protein and glucose, it comes from the bloodstream and is filtered by ventricles within the brain.

Cerebrum The two hemispheres of the brain connected by the corpus collosum.

Chromosome A string of DNA that contains instructions for a range of developments. Each human cell contains 46 chromosomes arranged in 23 pairs.

Cognition The higher order functions, including speech, reasoning, logical thought, memorising, attention and perception.

Cooing An early stage in making sounds from about one to four months when vowels are repeated.

Corpus collosum The thick band of fibres connecting the right and left hemispheres of the brain where impulses pass to involve both sides in facilitating actions and thoughts.

Cortex The convoluted grey matter of the brain made up of a 4mm thick band of neurones that govern thinking.

Cortisol A hormone necessary for survival. It regulates blood pressure and the use of sugars and proteins. In times of stress it provides an emergency source of energy. If it stays in the brain too long, it can overwhelm rational thinking and cause reactions to be aggressive.

Critical times A time during development when the child is especially responsive to particular kinds of perception and learning. Although educators must believe that it is never too late to learn, it is harder, even much harder to acquire the same skills at times outwith the critical period.

Dendrites The thin branches of a neuron that receive impulses from terminal fibres at the synapse and carry them into the neuron. They develop rapidly in the last three prenatal months and in the first year after birth.

Dialogic reading A type of reading in which the adult poses questions and where the answers are not contained in the pictures but deduction is required. Children thus educated showed greater vocabulary and comprehension scores.

Down's syndrome A condition caused by incorrect cell division so that each cell has three copies of chromosome 21 rather than two. Some intellectual delay and specific physical features are part of this syndrome.

Dyspraxia A specific learning difference in which the planning and execution of motor patterns causes difficulty. Children are mostly of average or above average intelligence with one aspect of development surprisingly low.

Efferent   Information from the central nervous system to the body.

Embryo   The developing organism from two to eight weeks after conception following implantation of the blastocyst into the uterine wall.

Endomorphins   Neurotransmitters that control pain and stimulate reward centres within the brain.

Equilibration   The third part of the adaptation process describing the restructuring of schema.

Extroversion   One of the key personality traits signifying outgoingness and confidence.

Fallopian tube   The tube between the ovary and the uterus where conception usually occurs.

Foetal alcohol syndrome   An extreme condition found in some newborns of alcoholic mothers. Low intelligence and flat facial features are part of this condition.

Frontal lobes   The largest lobes of the cerebral cortex. The front part is concerned with learning, personality and behaviour, while the back part controls voluntary movement.

GABA   Or gamma aminobutyric acid is the most important inhibitory neurotransmitter in the brain. It controls the number of messages that are sent at the same time to prevent fitting.

Gametes   The sperm and ova that contain only 23 chromosomes rather than 23 pairs.

Genotype   The genotype is the unique genetic blueprint that characterises each individual.

Glial cells   These form the bulk of the brain – there are many more glial cells than neurons. They feed and repair the brain and are the source of myelin.

Grey matter   The part of the brain where neurons (thinking cells) are found.

Hemispheres   The right and left hemispheres comprise the cerebrum. Each is divided into four lobes: the occipital, the temporal, the parietal and the frontal lobe. Each has specific dominant functions but they work together through the corpus collosum to facilitate thought and action.

Hippocampus   Part of the temporal lobe involved with learning and memory. It forms part of the limbic system.

Hypothalamus   Part of the limbic system that regulates the production of hormones. It helps control temperature, food intake and heart rate.

Infant directed speech   The formal name for motherese, the higher pitched musical communications that adults in this culture use instinctively with children.

Intelligence quotient or IQ   A measure of a child's ability on certain tasks compared to many others in the age group.

Limbic system   A group of structures around the edge of the brain stem that are associated with memory, learning and emotional processing. Currently its function is being debated.

Low birth weight   The name given to any baby born below 5½lb (2,500g). This includes pre-term babies and those who are small for date.

Maturation   The sequential unfolding of physical and intellectual characteristics contained in the genetic code.

Medulla oblongata   The lower part of the brain stem that relays information between the brain and the spinal cord.

Meiosis   The process within gamete division wherein each new cell receives only one chromosome from each original pair. So each gamete has only 23 chromosomes, not 23 pairs.

Memory   Different types are: remote, which recalls long past events; working, which allows the recall of actions just past; procedural, which stores practised actions that can be recalled, e.g. riding a bike; and prospective memory, which allows recall of a planned event.

Motherese   See infant directed speech.

Myelin   A fatty sheath (composed of glial cells) that insulates most axons. This sheath is not fully developed at birth and there are specific times when there is a surge. It feeds and supports the axons and can be built up through movement activity. Myelin is lost in diseases such as multiple sclerosis.

Nerve fibres   These are axons that extend from the body of the cell and transmit the impulses from one to the other. Afferent fibres take the stimulus towards the cell and efferent fibres carry it away. In groups they form nerve bundles.

Neuron   The thinking cell responsible for the reception and transmission of nerve impulses.

Neurotransmitters   Chemicals that respond to the electrical charge to take the impulse across the synapse. About 50 of these chemicals work to excite or inhibit the impulse. Each has a different function.

Oestrogen   The female sex hormone secreted by the ovaries.

Ovum   The female gamete which, if fertilised by a sperm from the male, combines to form the foetus.

Peripheral nervous system   The nerves outside the central nervous system that connect to muscles, skin and joints.

Permanence   The understanding that an object or person does not disappear when they are out of sight. An important part of bonding. The trust that the carer will return.

Personality   A group of relatively enduring ways of viewing and reacting to people and events in the world. Temperament is the emotional substrate of personality.

Phenotype   The expression of genetic material in a specific environment.

Placenta   This organ develops during gestation. It filters nutrients from the mother's blood and acts as kidneys, liver and lungs for the developing foetus.

Positron emission topography (PET)   A scanning procedure that illuminates how parts of the brain are functioning.

Proprioceptors   are the nerve endings that cover every part of the body. They receive information from the senses and work to give a sense of 'place' or body awareness in space.

Proteins   Compounds made up of amino acids that control the way the cells function.

Proximodistal   One of the two basic processes in physical development (the other is cephalocaudal) that describes the increase in bodily strength moving from the centre or core of the body to the edge or periphery. This explains why finger control develops late.

Receptive language   The child's ability to receive and understand language, as opposed to speaking it.

Reflexes   Automatic body reactions to a stimulus. Primitive reflexes should be washed away to let postural reflexes take their place. Some adaptive reflexes remain throughout life.

Resilience   A personality or temperamental trait that allows children and adults to be positive – to see the sunny side of events.

Rubella   A form of measles that, if contracted during the first three months of pregnancy, is likely to affect the baby's sight and hearing.

Schema A Piagetan term for a number of basic patterns of behaviour. Physical actions come under the term 'sensori-motor schemas'. Experiences are assimilated into schemas and modified through accommodation.

Sense of gender The appreciation of one's own gender, including understanding of constancy and permanency of gender.

Social referencing Using another person's non-verbal communication to make decisions about actions, e.g. if the parent is frowning or appears tense, the toddler may desist.

Strange situations A series of experiments designed by Ashworth to test babies' responses on the return of absent parents. On that basis, she determined whether or not children were securely attached.

Synapse The space between the terminal fibres of one axon and the receiving dendrites of another. Impulses are passed by chemicals called neurotransmitters, e.g. dopamine.

Synchrony A complex pattern of interactions where trust builds up and expectations are met.

Temperament The emotional part of the personality, partially determined by the genes.

Teratogens Harmful substances that significantly increase the risk of prenatal deviations and abnormalities.

Thalamus The centre above the brain stem that relays information from the cortex to the sensory organs such as retina, the skin and the inner ear.

Umbilical cord The cord that connects the embryo/foetus' circulatory system to the placenta. The tube carries nutrients and eliminates waste.

Uterus The female recipient of the blastocyst. The area (womb) where the baby develops. The baby's first environment.

Vestibular sense or sense of balance is the first sense to be developed. Since all other sensory information passes through the vestibular sense it has a profound effect on learning. It is in the inner ear with the auditory sense. Babies who require a breech birth may have a poor sense of balance because their vestibular sense has not got them into the correct head down position for a vaginal birth.

White matter The myelinated neural fibres and glial cells that make up most of the central nervous system.

Williams syndrome is caused by a genetic mutation that produces retardation with extraordinary linguistic skill. The affected person speaks fluently and at length but the conversation lacks meaning, is contextually irrelevant and not likely to improve. IQ tends to be between 50 and 70.

References

Aaron, J. (2006) NFAT Increased Dosage of DSCR11 and DYRKIA on Chromosome 21. *Nature*, 441: 595–9.

Apgar, V.A. (1953) A Proposal for a New Method of Evaluation on the Newborn Infant. *Current Research in Anasthesia and Analgesia*, 32: 260–7.

Ainsworth, M.D.S. (1972) Attachment and Dependency: A comparison, in J.L. Gewirtz (ed.), *Attachment and Dependency*. Washington, DC: V.H. Winston, pp. 97–138.

Bandura A. (1989) Social Cognitive Theory. *Annals of Child Development*, 6: 1–60.

Bates, E., Bretherton, I. and Snyder, L. (1988) *From First Words to Grammar: Individual differences and dissociable mechanisms*. Cambridge: Cambridge University Press.

BBC (2005) *Baby It's You*. Lezayre: Beckmann Visual Publishing.

Bee, H. (1995) *The Developing Child* (7th edn). New York: HarperCollins.

Bee, H. and Boyd, D. (2005) *The Developing Child* (international edn). Boston, MA: Pearson Publications.

Bennett, R. V. and Brown, L.K. (1989) *Myles Textbook for Midwives*. Edinburgh: Churchill Livingstone.

Best Practice Network (2010) *EYPS Standards: Skills for caring and development*. Bristol: Best Practice Network.

Bialystock, E., Shenfield, T. and Codd, J. (1997) Effects of Bilingualism and Bilateracy on Children's Emerging Concepts of Print. *Developmental Psychology*, 33.

Bigler, R.S. (1995) The Role of Classification Skill in Moderating Environmental Influences on Children's Gender Stereotyping: A study of the functional use of gender in the classroom. *Child Development*, 66: 1072–87.

Brody, N. (1992) *Intelligence* (2nd edn). San Diego, CA: Academic Press.

Carter, R. (2000) *Mapping the Mind*. London: Phoenix Books.

Children's Workforce Development Council (2008) *Early Years Professional Status*. Ormskirk: Edgehill University.

City of Edinburgh Council (2008) *A Curriculum for Excellence*. Edinburgh.

Collins, M. (2005) *It's OK to be Sad*. Bristol: Lucky Duck Publishing.

Dixon, P. (2005) *Let Me Be: A cry for the rights of creativity and childhood in education*. Peche Luna Press.

Dowling, M. (2004). *Young Children's Personal, Social and Emotional Development*. London: Paul Chapman Publishing.

Epstein, S. (1991) Cognitive-experiential Self-theory: Implications for developmental psychology, in M.R. Gunner and L.A. Sroufe (eds), *The Minnesota Symposia on Child Development*, 23: 79–123.

Fagot, B.I. (1995) Parenting Boys and Girls, in M.H. Bornstein (ed.) *Handbook of Parenting, Vol. 1, Children and Parenting*, pp. 163–83. Mahwah, NJ: Lawrence Erlbaum Publishers.

Fenson, L. (1994) Variability in Early Communicative Development. *Monographs of the Society for Research in Child Development*, 59: 242.

Gagne, R. (2001) A Model for Giftedness and Talent, in *A Framework for Giftedness and Talent*. Edinburgh City Council.

Gardner, H. (1983) *Frames of Mind: The theory of multiple intelligences*. New York. Basic Books.

Gardner, H. (2007) *Five Minds for the Future*. Cambridge, MA: Harvard University Press.

Goddard, S. (1996) *A Teacher's Window into the Child's Mind*. Eugene, OR: Fern Ridge Press.

Goddard Blythe, S. (2008) *What Babies and Children Really Need*. Stroud: Hawthorn Press Early Years Series.

Goodenough, F.L. (1972) *Anger in Young Children*. Minneapolis, MN: University of Minnesota Press.

Hawley, T.L. and Disney, E.R. (1992) *Crack's Children: The consequences of maternal cocaine abuse*. Social Policy Report, Society for Research in Child Development 6 (4): 1–22.

Hollich, G. (2000) Breaking the Language Barrier: An emergentist coalition model for the origins of word learning. *Monographs of the Society of Research in Child Development*, 65: 1–123.

Horowitz, F. D. (1987) *Exploring Developmental Theories: Towards a structural/behavioural model of development*. Hillsdale, NJ: Erlbaum.

Hubbard, F.O.A. and van Ijzendoorn, M.H. (1997) The Relationships Between Cry Characteristics, Demographic Variables and Developmental Test Scores. *Infant Behaviour and Development*, 13: 533–8.

Hughes, A. M. (2010) *Developing Play for the Under 3s* (2nd edn). Oxon: David Fulton Publishers.

Huntington, L., Hans, S.L. and Zeskind, P.S. (1990) The Relations Among the Cry Characteristics, Demographic Variables and Developmental Test Scores in Infants Prenatally Exposed to Methadone. *Infant Behaviour and Development*, 13: 533–8.

Huttenlocher, J. (1998) Language Input and Language Growth. *Preventative Medicine*, 27: 195–9.

Isaacs, S. (1933) *Social Development in Young Children*. London: Routledge.

Keen, C.L. and Hurely, L.S. (1989) Zinc and Reproduction: Effects of deficiency on foetal and post-natal development, in C.F. Mills (ed.) *Zinc in Human Biology*. London: Springer-Verlag, pp. 183–220.

Kirby, A. (1999) *Dyspraxia: The hidden handicap*. London: Souvenir Press.

Lee, K. (2010) *Little Liars Grow up to be Great Leaders*. Research report: Institute of Child Study, Toronto University Press.

Maccoby, E.E. and Martin, J.A. (1983) Socialisation in the Context of the Family: Parent–child interaction, in P.H. Mussen and E.M. Hetherington (ed.) *Handbook of Child Psychology: Socialisation, personality, and social development, Vol. 4*. New York: Wiley, pp. 1–102.

McCune, L. (1995) A Normative Study of Representational Play at the Transition to Language. *Developmental Psychology*, 31: 198–206.

Macintyre, C. (2002a) *The Art of Action Research in the Classroom*. Oxon: David Fulton Publishers.

Macintyre, C. (2002b) *Early Intervention in Movement*. Oxon: David Fulton Publishers.

Macintyre, C. (2009) *Bullying and Young Children*. Oxon: David Fulton Publishers.

Macintyre, C. (2010) *Play for Children with Special Needs* (2nd edn). Oxon: David Fulton Publishers.

Macintyre, C. (2011) *Enhancing Learning through Play: A developmental perspective for early years settings*. Oxon: Routledge.

Macintyre, C. and Murdoch, E. (1986) Unpublished research. Dunfermline College of Physical Education, Edinburgh.

Messer, D. (1994) *The Development of Communication from Social Interaction to Language*. Chichester: Wiley.

Moore, C. (2004) *George and Sam*. London: Viking.

Moore, K.L. and Persaud, T.V.N. (1993) *The Developing Human: Clinically oriented embryology* (5th edn) Philadelphia, PA: Saunders.

Patterson, G.R. (1996) Some Characteristics of a Developmental Theory for Early-onset Delinquency, in M.F. Lenzenweger and J.J. Haugaard (eds) *Frontiers of Developmental Psychopathology*, Oxford: Oxford University Press, pp. 81–124.

Piaget, J. (1952) *The Origins of Intelligence in Children*. New York: International Universities Press.

Pinker, S. (1987) The Bootstrapping Problem in Language Acquisition, in B. McWhinney (ed.) *Mechanisms of Language Acquisition*. Hillsdale, NJ: Lawrence Erlbaum, pp. 399–442.

Pinker, S. (1994) *The Language Instinct: How the mind creates language*. New York: William Morrow.

Robinson, M. (2010) *Understanding Behaviour and Development in Early Childhood*. London: Routledge.

Robinson, M. (2011) Attachment as a Process. Paper presented at the Kirklees Early Years Conference, Huddersfield.

Slobin, D.I. (ed.) *The Crosslinguistic Study of Language Acquisition. Vol. 2, Theoretical Issues*. Hillsdale, NJ: Lawrence Erlbaum, pp. 1157–256.

Snow, C.E. (1997) Cross-domain Connections and Social Class Differences: Two challenges to non-environmental views of language development. Paper presented at the Conference on Child Development, Washington, DC.

Sroufe, L.A., Carlsen, E. and Shulman, S. (1993) Individuals in Relationships: Development from infancy to adolescence, in D.C. Funder, R.D. Parke, C. Tomlinson-Keasey and K. Widamen (eds) *Studying Lives through Time: Personality and development*. Washington, DC: American Psychological Association, pp. 315–42.

Sternberg, R.J. (1985) *Beyond IQ: A Triarchic theory of human intelligence*. New York: Cambridge University Press.

Sutherland, M. (2006) The Key Relational Needs of the Child. Paper presented at the Early Years Conference, Bolden.

Tanner, J.M. (1990) *Foetus into Man* (revised and enlarged edition). Cambridge, MA: Harvard University Press.

Thelen, E. (1981) Rhythmical Behaviour in Infancy: An ethological perspective. *Developmental Psychology*, 17: 237–57.

Thomas, A. and Chess, S. (1977) *Temperament and Development*. New York: Brunner/Mazel Publishers.

Thomson, P.M. (2001) Genetic Influences on Brain Structure. *Nature Neuroscience*, 4: 1253–8.

Trevarthen, C. (1977) *Play for Tomorrow*. Edinburgh University video production.

Ukeje, I., Bendersky, M. and Lewis, M. (2001) Mother/Infant Interaction at 12 Months in Prenatally Cocaine Exposed Children. *American Journal of Drug and Alcohol Abuse*, 27: 203–24.

Whitehurst, G.J., Falco, F.L. and Lonigan, C.J. (1998) Accelerating Language Through Picture Book Reading. *Developmental Psychology*, 24: 552–9.

Winkley, D. (2004) Grey Matters: Current neurological research and its implications for educators. Seminar www.keele.ac.uk/depts/ed/kisnet/interviews/winkley.htm.

Winston, R. (2004) *The Human Mind and How to Make the Most of It*. London: Bantam Books.

Index